How to Stay Christian

John Galloway, Jr.

Judson Press ® Valley Forge

HOW TO STAY CHRISTIAN

Library of Congress Cataloging in Publication Data
Galloway, John T.
How to stay Christian.
Includes bibliographical references.
1. Christian life—1960- . 2. Bible. N.T. John XV—Criticism, interpretation, etc. I. Title.
BV4501.2.G324 1984 248.4 84-9725
ISBN 0-8170-1038-6

Printed in the U.S.A.

to
My Father

Preface

Being Christian is not an individual way of life. Christianity is not a solo flight. It is always a team effort.

Being Christian is being in touch . . . with God . . . with Christian tradition . . . with the body of Christ, which is the church.

Staying Christian, then, is staying in touch through the community of believers who support us, hassle us, comfort us, annoy us, surprise us with their caring, disappoint us with their carelessness, challenge us, prod us, and through it all surround us with the presence of Christ.

Bringing this manuscript to its present form has been for me a living parable of what I hope the manuscript itself is all about. The book is a product of my being and staying in touch . . . with the Lord in prayer . . . with church tradition through enough commentaries to create a two-foot high wall on my desk top . . . and with the marvelous company of believers I have been privileged to know.

I want to thank the congregation of the First Presbyterian Church of York. It was there that I began to work through John 15 in a six-week sermon series. With apologies to the good saints of York, I must confess that it was not until the Friday before the last sermon in the series was to be delivered that it dawned on me that John 15 is really a study about how to stay Christian. By then it was too late. I could not invite the congregation back to sit through messages one through five preached to the beat of a different drum. So I figured if I ever got called to a new parish, I'd do John 15 from scratch, and do it in the light of its proper theme.

In October of 1980 I did one of the most difficult things I have ever done. I left the great fellowship of York. With John 15 notes, the only thing I would not let the movers pack, tucked under my arm I headed west. Memories came along: memories of Catherine Sweitzer typing notes long after my sermon series had been delivered; of Betty Schonauer reviewing what I had written on the first few chapters of John 15 and offering her excellent advice; of eight wonderful years surrounded by a tremendous congregation.

I arrived at Fox Chapel Presbyterian Church where I began collecting more and more commentaries and sermons on John 15. After just a few months, the "new minister" sprung a sixteen-week sermon series on the unsuspecting flock. As testimony to their patience and stamina, the church is still there.

I have been richly blessed by these two congregations, by countless study groups that have given me feedback on John 15, by radio audiences, youth retreats, and officer training events—all hearing about how to stay Christian in the light of the vine and the branches.

Special thanks go to my secretary at Fox Chapel, Betty Wilcox, for typing and retyping my meanderings; and to Linda Payne for typing the final draft and introducing me to no-cal, no-caffeine soda pop. Roland Tapp has been of tremendous help to me over the years, particularly on this project, offering advice and aiding in bringing about publication. The Lord has kept me in touch with good people.

My wife, Susan, and children, Scott, Christie, and Katherine, deserve medals for putting up with me while a manuscript kept me from them.

And a word of gratitude to my father to whom this book is dedicated. He has always demonstrated to me the art of staying Christian. He also has an unusual gift of being able to give me encouragement without letting my ego get too large for my own good. After reviewing my last rough draft, he suggested I pursue the venture for publication. "You think it's okay?" I asked, fishing for a compliment. "Parts of it aren't too bad," he said. I was pleased. Besides, humility is a necessary part of staying Christian.

John Galloway, Jr.
Fox Chapel Presbyterian Church
Pittsburgh, Pennsylvania
April 1984

Contents

INTRODUCTION

Keeping Active Church Members Active

"I have said all this to you to keep you from falling away" (John 16:1).

A woman sits in her pastor's study, occasionally dabbing reddened eyes with wadded tissues. "I've lost my faith," she sobs. She had wondered if she would be able to say that to her pastor, and now she has. These words spoken, the rest come more easily. "I can't understand what has happened to me. I have tried to live a Christian life. I still attend church programs. You see me almost every Sunday, though I admit I'm slipping a bit lately in that department. But I feel like I'm just going through empty motions. The spark I once had is gone."

A leading family in the church, the kind of people you always count on at congregational activities, suddenly stops appearing. When a caller from the church inquires, the family members claim (however honestly) that nothing is wrong. They love the church and always will. However, when the youngest child went off to college, they found themselves drifting into a different life-style with different priorities. Maybe they will get back to church. But not for a while.

A man loses his job, feels he cannot keep his financial commitment to the church, and drops out.

A teenager has a life-changing experience which makes the Lord real in a special new way. For a time the youngster moves from fellowship to fellowship, sharing a powerful though probably undigested testimony. Then, all of a sudden, it stops. Old habits creep in. The excitement of faith disappears, leaving nothing of lasting value.

These are examples of an all-too-common occurrence in church life. Statistics reveal that at least one-third of the persons whose names are on the roll of the average local church are inactive. Discipleship that was once alive and vibrant has become dormant or dead.

We have seen so much of it, we take it for granted. As with the bad news that comes to us in the morning paper or evening news broadcast, we find ourselves growing immune to the tragedy of misplaced faith. We actually begin to assume that people will lose their faith. It seems normal. Many churches schedule their corporate activities (church school, worship, special services) on the premise that a majority of members will stay away.

Take the matter of Sunday morning worship, for example. Many churches would find that if they multiplied the seating capacity of their worship centers by the number of services conducted, the total would fall far short of their membership. It is not unusual for a church with 1,600 members to hold two services Sunday morning in a 400-seat sanctuary. It is assumed that 800 or fewer persons will attend each week. Were all the members of the church to choose a particular Sunday to show up for worship, it would be madness. Easter's overflow would pale in comparison. Worshipers would be turned away for lack of room. Such churches not only assume inactivity, they expect it.

Sadly, the expectation is well founded. People have been drifting away from the faith for centuries. One contemporary humorist asked the morbid question: "Do you ever look at a crowd scene from a 1935 movie and wonder how many of those people are alive today?" A query more relevant to our topic would be, "Do you ever look at a congregation and wonder how many of them will still be spiritually alive next year?" The chances are good that several of them will not be. Do you ever look at a class of young people confessing their faith to unite with the church and wonder how many of them will mature into adult Christians, to say nothing of maintaining their faith for one more year?

In recent years programs have been developed to reach out to our lost sheep and bring them back. Some church leaders are suggesting that the most fertile field for evangelism lies within our own membership rolls. Others advise that the future vitality of the community requires creative involvement of the marginal members. So-called inactive church members are fast becoming the number-one target for ministry, and it is about time.

As the pastor of a local congregation, I am supportive of efforts to reach persons whose faith has slipped and who have drifted from involvement. I am doubly pleased when a man like Dr. John Savage, perhaps the most skilled individual in the field of ministry to inactives, includes in his workshops guidance as to how to recognize and reach persons who are on the verge of becoming inactive. In other words, he teaches preventive maintenance. Therein lies our theme.

I write in the conviction that it is possible for us who are inside the faith and who believe our faith is reasonably healthy—not perfect, mind you, but healthy—to understand the spiritual forces that challenge our faith. I believe that when we begin to drift aimlessly away, there is something that can snap us back. Resources are available. When we come upon a barrier, there is a Power to see us through. There are steps I can follow to be in touch with that Power. Resources are available. This book is written in the assurance that a careful study of John 15 will inject spiritual stamina into our veins.

When John R. Mott, an early leader in the YMCA, was a little boy, his mother told him, "The greatest chapter in the whole Bible is the fifteenth chapter of John." That insight and subsequent reliance of Jesus' teaching in that "greatest" chapter led Mott to a lifelong ministry of service. John 15 gives ammunition, perspective, and words to remember in our hours of testing. Anyone who wants to stay Christian needs a full dose of John 15.

By way of introduction, let's set the scene. Let's go back almost two thousand years to Jerusalem, get to know the setting of this famous chapter, drink in the atmosphere, and see how fear of the disciples' becoming inactive played on the Lord's mind. In other words, let's investigate the notion that the "greatest chapter in the whole Bible" was prompted by Christ's desire that you and I and all his disciples stay Christian.

We learn that the well-to-do in David's city could afford a second story to their homes, an open, spacious room for entertaining guests. Jesus had grown close to one such homeowner and made arrangements for His disciples to celebrate the Passover upstairs in the homeowner's house. We call it simply "The Upper Room." It was a room to which the disciples would flee in fear the next afternoon after Jesus had been killed. It was a room into which the risen Christ would mysteriously come to bless and send out the faithful. But this night it was for eating the Passover meal, for summing up the years, for making sure the disciples had caught the message and it had stuck. Would they be ready for what was about to happen? Would they have the spiritual glue to stick to it after Jesus was gone? Or would the challenges of discipleship cause them to drift away?

John's transcription of what was said during this farewell address, or last discourse, as it is called, leaves the reader with an odd impression. Reading the thirteenth through the seventeenth chapters of John, one might have expected to find Jesus comforting his loyal followers as they faced the trauma of Good Friday. "Let not your hearts be troubled," (John 14:1) would have seemed an apt theme for the Lord's remarks. I expected to find Jesus trying to inspire these folk, seeking to pick up the spirits of his pupils. Beneath the challenges of the hour, one might have anticipated an atmosphere in which people relied on one another as they faced a common challenge.

Instead, we find suspicion hanging in the air. Jesus' words reveal that he had a grave concern that these well-trained troops might not have been schooled well enough. They might not have developed what it takes to remain loyal when the realities of life hit. They might not be ready. They might fall away. They might become the first names on the long list of persons who would become inactive through the centuries of Christian history. Come to think of it, if these few followers had dropped out, would there have been a Christian history?

In both chapters 13 and 14, Jesus had stated that he was offering words for the presently faithful to store away in their memory banks for that difficult hour when their faith would be strained (John 13:19 and 14:29). The opening line in chapter 16 reads, "I have said all this to you to keep you from falling away" (John 16:1). Though these words specifically refer back only to the last verses of chapter 15, in a general sense they do more than that. They come from the heart of Jesus' final discourse, interpreting the whole. John 16:1, not John 14:1, is the theme of the evening. Throughout this final meeting before Calvary, Jesus drummed home insights and spiritual thought-starters to keep the disciples from falling away into inactivity.

Think of that! Mind you, these were not idle hangers-on to whom he was speaking. These were the people who had stayed with him when hundreds, perhaps thousands, had turned their backs and walked away. Judas had slipped out, but Jesus did not change his attitude as if Iscariot were the only one susceptible to falling. The very ones who had proved their loyalty were the ones to whom he voiced his concern. They had been in a three-year intensive clinic with the Lord. Their consciousness had constantly been raised. They had grown accustomed to the timbre of his voice. From firsthand experience they knew what it was to be in a tight scrape and have Jesus miraculously deliver them. They had seen the blinking, wide-eyed wonder of a person whose sight had been restored. They had seen the blank, confused blush on the faces of the best minds of the day caught in mental checkmate by the carpenter from Nazareth. They had been there. They had been with the Man. They had watched Him. And, after all that, Jesus was afraid they might lose their faith.

Think about that! If Jesus worried about those loyal devotees who could buttress their faith with the fact of having seen him in the flesh, how he must wonder about those of us who have not seen and yet believe! (John 20:29).

No Christian dare take his or her faith for granted. Any one of us could lose faith. We could lose it overnight, or watch it erode, eaten away by the sands of time. When Jesus said, "I have said all this to you to keep you from falling away," he was not only speaking to the guests gathered in the Upper Room, but was also reaching across the ages to us, because he does not want us to fall away, and he knows we might.

He wants us to stay Christian and he tells us how. Perseverance is the point of his last discourse, the purpose behind John 15. Our Lord invites us to launch a program of preventive maintenance in our churches, our homes, our individual lives. We don't have to become inactive church members, persons who lost faith, who fell away. We can build endurance through spiritual training in a program Jesus laid out in that Upper Room.

CHAPTER 1

Where to Begin

"I am . . ." (John 15:1).

Someone once said that a journey of a thousand miles begins with a single step. Who could disagree with that marvelous advice? What the sage who uttered the wisdom failed to tell us, however, is what that single step might be. How do we launch ourselves as Christians into a plan to keep the faith? Where do we begin? Where do we start?

A number of possible starting points rush to mind. Prayer and Bible study have nourished the faithful for centuries. Why not clear time on the daily calendar so that devotions can claim a definite space in our busy schedules? Or we could come at it from another angle. In this impersonal society nothing tops good wholesome Christian fellowship. One could seek out a small group sharing the gospel, supporting one another in love, offering strength for the down times, and keeping us humble when times are good. Or who among us does not need discipline? Perhaps a program to sustain faith could commence with a resolution about life-style: regular church attendance, tithing, taking less for ourselves so that we can share more with God's children who are less fortunate than we are.

Though the list could go on and on, no one can fault the qualities already noted. Each could deepen spiritual life and lead to a dynamic church, blessed by the Lord. All of them ought to be habits naturally built into Christian living. As a pastor, I wish I could single them out as musts for starting down the path of Christian perseverance. But I cannot. A biblically based regimen would not allow it.

If we want to stay Christian, there is only one place to begin: Begin with Jesus Christ.

Immediately questions pop up: "How?" "What am I supposed to do?" "What steps do I follow in beginning with Jesus?" Since we Christians are extremely eager to do what is right, the questions demand quick and ready answers. When our Christian ears pick up the words "Begin with Jesus Christ," something jogs the spiritual computer in our hearts, making us want to jump up and do something. We like the sound of beginning with Christ. We want to get on with it. We want to know what to do.

Unfortunately, our apparently best motives have a way of leading us occasionally in the wrong direction. We romp off toward some goal, only to find that inadvertently we have put ourselves in the wrong lane. Good intentions can have bad destinations. Such is the case here.

When our hearing is excited by the notion of beginning with Christ, we should do nothing. Despite our eager enthusiasm (or maybe because of it), we should let the matter rest for a time, give it room, calm ourselves down. While it sounds like the height of folly to begin an important program by doing nothing, there is absolutely no other way.

The very asking of the question "What am I supposed to do?" defeats the purpose of beginning with Christ. Wondering what I am supposed to do, by definition, begins with "me." "I" am the subject. "I" am the one who is to do whatever it is determined has to be done. Jesus fades into the clouded recesses of my unconscious mind, while "I" self-righteously rack my brain thinking about "myself" and what "I" might do. To begin with Christ, let's not ask how. Christ is the point; that is all.

In 1962 a seminary professor concluded an article with this Christ-centered paragraph:

> We talk a great deal *about* God and *about* Christ, but if we are to know "what it means to be saved," then we are summoned to listen to the first-person words spoken to us. George McLeod says that "I" is the most dangerous word we use, and I suspect that is true. But to listen to God speaking is another matter. "I am the Lord your God," "I am with you," "I will help you," "I have sent my son for you"—to listen to Christ speaking His great "I am's" to us is to be delivered from our selves that we may find our selves. For these are saving words for us.[1]

Jesus chose his words carefully as he spoke to the anxious audience huddled in the Upper Room. He knew that what he said would be remembered by the disciples as they faced moments of crisis in the future. His words would lie at the heart and form the substance of their plan to stay Christian. So, when he launched into that section of his remarks which the church has designated as John 15, he wanted to begin at the right place. What better two-word combination could he have chosen than "I am"? He focused attention on himself because he is the starting point.

We run into the term "I am" first in the Old Testament book of Exodus, in the well-known tale of Moses at the burning bush (Exodus 3). While tending his father-in-law's flock, Moses noticed a bush engulfed in flames but not being burned up by it. If that were not enough for one day, Moses heard the voice of God speaking to him out of the bush, instructing him to go down into Egypt and lead the Jewish people out.

Now Moses was a planner. His mind raced ahead. He knew that when he arrived on the scene in Egypt and began his community organization, the people would raise some legitimate questions. They would want to know on what authority Moses had come. In that age when many gods were worshiped, they would want to know the name of the God who was standing behind him. To be ready for what he knew would be a question thrown at him, Moses asked the voice in the bush to identify itself by name. God responded by saying simply, "Yahweh." One of the most powerful names for the Lord in the Old Testament was the word "Yahweh." It means "I am who I am," or, more briefly, "I am." Evidently Moses was content with that as he did not press his interrogation any further. "I am" was enough. He would accept that.

When Jesus said, "I am," as he did several times in John's Gospel, He was uttering a term that brought the full presence of the Old Testament God into the New Testament situation. He was saying, in effect, "The power of the God who brought our people out of Egypt is here in this room." To begin with Jesus saying, "I am," is to be drawn into the presence of almighty God.

Jesus used the "I am" phrase to usher in an analogy. He moved quickly past "I am" to his teaching about the vine: "I am the true vine." As we will discuss more fully in chapter 4, Jesus is the One who genuinely feeds us, who is our spiritual life support system, just as a vine is for its branches. The analogy invites us to pursue it. But before we do, we would be wise to mull over those well-used first two words.

John often recalled Jesus saying, "I am." In Christian tradition the words themselves have had an identity and a meaning. Through the years, many preachers have delivered sermon series on Jesus' "I am" sayings. We do not abuse the intent of John 15 by fixing for a moment on "I am" any more than we violate the creation story by freezing the flow for an instant on the phrase "In the beginning God. . . . "

The first step in staying Christian is to hear these two words: "I am." Definitions are set aside. Human effort is at rest. We do not define the moment or even describe what it is to be in God's presence. We simply know we are with him. He is Lord. He lives. He is in touch with us. "I am," he said. The reality of God, rather than thoughts about him, is what provides our refuge and strength, our light and our salvation.

When I was a youngster, I memorized what many people consider the best definition of God ever written. It is in the *Shorter Catechism of the Westminster Confession of Faith*, and it reads: "God is a Spirit, infinite, eternal, and unchangeable, in his being, wisdom, power, holiness, justice, goodness, and truth." I could spout for anyone at a moment's notice the answer to the question "What is God?" To this day I believe God cannot be better defined. But to this day I have never prayed to that definition, nor has that definition been with me in any one of life's dark hours of loneliness or bright flashes of inspiration. The definition merely talks *about* the One who has been there, the One who is, the One who said, "I am." The power of the Lord comes out of the undefined awareness that God is alive. Prayer comes to life not so much as well-chosen words are offered to a neatly defined deity but as a heartfelt murmuring to the One who is. Let's not start the program by thinking *about* God. Let us build on the knowledge that we are in his presence.

Generations ago Jonathan Dickinson argued that theological doctrines and confessions are made by people. They are the result of persons prayerfully or not so prayerfully deducing or inducing principles from what Scripture says. While there is certainly a valid place for doctrinal truth in our faith, it is not the place to begin, nor is it the place to rest our discipleship. Beneath all doctrines and definitions is the One who is.

Have you ever been in a discussion with a person who is disclaiming the Christian faith? The person will spew out all kinds of reasons why God cannot be believed, all the reasons why our concept of God has to be mistaken. To my surprise, the more the person talks, the more I seem to agree with what is being said, a rather awkward moment for a clergyman. But it can't be helped. The fact is I don't believe in *that* God either. The poor person has carried the burden of great doubt for some time. But the doubt has been about a particular definition of the deity rather than the reality of the Lord himself. Sometimes we have to cut through the humanly designed definitions to bask in the presence of the great "I Am."

Many college campuses have professors in the philosophy or religion departments who take some pride in the ease with which they can destroy the Christian religion. Faithful Christian students shudder at how routinely belief seems to evaporate in the heat of one semester with these wizards of nihilism. To survive such courses, students need to be able to spot a fundamental flaw in the technique commonly used. The first classes are usually spent putting the professor's understanding of the Christian religion on the chalkboard. The students will be asked if the statements on the board are accurate, and for the most part they are. The definitions and doctrines have been written in a way showing that the professor understands the subject, while drawing the believing student into an emotional attachment to what the chalk has left on the board. The professor will then spend the rest of the course systematically destroying what was written down at the beginning. Since the students figured Christianity had been put on the board, destroying the board would seem to destroy Christianity. Not so. The essence of our faith can never be reduced to a chalkboard. Only thoughts about it can. The essence of our faith is the God who lives and who is with us even when people far smarter than we are poke holes in our religious definitions. We begin our program not with a tenacious clinging to doctrine but with Job's simple affirmation, "I know that my Redeemer lives" (Job 19:25).

Harry Emerson Fosdick told this story in one of his sermons:

> They say that a Russian girl took a government examination under the Soviet *régime* and, after the examination was over, feared she might have failed. In particular she worried about one question—"What is the inscription on the Sarmian wall?" She had written down what she thought it was—"Religion is the opiate of the people"—but after she was through with the examination she walked seven miles from Leningrad to the Sarmian wall to be sure. There it was just as she had written, "Religion is the opiate of the people." Then falling upon her knees she crossed herself and said, "Thank God!"[2]

Beneath all the slogans, all the philosophizing, all the definitions, and even behind all the neat arguments why he doesn't exist, God continues to be the One who can say "I am."

When I told my father that I planned to begin my discussion of how to stay Christian with a chapter on "I am," and that I planned to draw on the word "Yahweh," he suggested that I look into a book written by William F. Albright. For years Albright had been professor of Semitic languages at Johns Hopkins University. In the book *From the Stone Age to Christianity,* he does indeed have something to enrich our understanding at this point. "Many different meanings have been attributed to *Yahweh* by scholars who recognized its relative antiquity, but only one yields any suitable sense: 'He causes to be.'" Albright argued that the "enigmatic formula" used at the burning bush means "I am what I am," but can easily be transposed into the third person, as is required by the causative "Yahweh." The phrase then means, "He Causes to be what Comes into Existence."[3]

This slant enriches our understanding because it means we begin our journey with the Source. All that happens to preserve our faith has its origin in Yahweh, the One who causes. Before you begin to read the next chapter, pause for a moment to think about Jesus, the One who said, "I am," the One who said, "I am the first and the last, the living one" (Revelation 1:17-18). He is the cause of which our faith is the effect. Dwell on him; dwell in him.

Notes

[1]James Muilenburg, "What I Believe It Means to Be Saved," *Union Seminary Quarterly Review*, vol. 17, no 4 (May, 1962), p. 293.

[2]Harry Emerson Fosdick, *Successful Christian Living* (New York: Harper & Row, Publishers Inc., 1937), p. 41.

[3]William F. Albright, *From the Stone Age to Christianity* (Baltimore: Johns Hopkins Press, 1940), p. 198.

CHAPTER 2

Have the Proper Perspective

"I am the true vine, and my Father is the vinedresser. Every branch of mine that bears no fruit, he takes away, and every branch that does bear fruit he prunes, that it may bear more fruit" (John 15:1-2).

If ever words were intended to pack a wallop, they are found in what Jesus said to his disciples a few hours before his arrest. The message is there for all to see, but until recently I had never really felt the brunt of it. Though imagery of a vinedresser, a vine, and the branches had long been a familiar part of my faith's landscape, I had not seen their meaning. I had unintentionally eluded the crunch of Jesus' teaching, while feeling quite smugly religious.

Perhaps of necessity my perspective is too far removed from that of Peter, Andrew, Matthew, or Philip. Instinctively they would have understood a vine as part of a man's trade, his means of livelihood. They would have known Jesus meant business. But my reactions have been conditioned differently. Gardens, vines, branches have always reminded me of leisure, puttering around in the yard after work. I have always had a sentimental attachment to John 15 because I felt the outdoors, the fresh breeze on my face. The language smacked of vacation, peace, comfort, relaxation, getting away from pressure and responsibility. "I am the true vine, and my Father is the vinedresser. Every branch of mine that bears no fruit, he takes away, and every branch that does bear fruit he prunes, that it may bear more fruit" (John 15:1-2). I could see these words in needlepoint, set against faded wallpaper on a kitchen wall adjacent to "Home Sweet Home." The verses sounded downright nice. It is embarrassing how words of our religious heritage can become so familiar to us and yet not communicate their intended message.

I have discovered that I liked this passage for the wrong reasons. Hearing it read, I thought the wrong thoughts. A chill of panic took hold of me when I realized what Jesus was actually saying, and I experienced a sense of humiliation at how obvious the meaning had been all along.

Wondering if I had been the only person to miss the point by so wide a margin, I conducted casual interviews with several friends, relatives, and colleagues to see if their perceptions had matched mine. I began by asking, "When you hear the words in John 15 about the vinedresser, the vine, and the branches, what do you see in your mind's eye?" The answers were a relief to my humbled ego.

One friend said, "I see a vine clinging to something which supports it as it grows . . . a wooden frame or something like that." When I asked where the vine was situated in relation to him, the reply was typical. "Well, it's over there (gesturing) about fifteen feet away." Someone else added to the picture: "The vinedresser is a skilled, efficient man, patiently scrutinizing his vine. He wears gray work clothes and his old shoes are wet from the morning dew. I see him walk over to the vine. From behind him, looking over his shoulder, I see him tenderly snip here and cut there, all for the good of the vine. He steps back to join me, cocking his head to one side as he looks at his work. He is finished."

Certain shared traits emerged from my poor man's Gallup Poll: (1) the majority of people felt this was a nonthreatening passage of Scripture; and (2) almost everyone shared a common perspective of standing with the vinedresser, then watching him walk "over there" to the vine some feet away.

While I took a touch of comfort in being with the majority, nothing could remove the sting of knowing that all of us were dead wrong about the intent of the passage. We had arrogantly put ourselves next to the vinedresser. We had opted to look at the scene from God's viewpoint, perhaps sipping lemonade while he did his work on others.

Jesus had a different perspective in store for us. He had intended our vision to be obscured by branches all around us, brushing against us. He wanted us to look from the inside out. We were hardly meant to be God's next-door neighbor dropping over to watch his Saturday morning gardening. Just the opposite. Each of us is to be one of the branches. To understand the opening verses of John 15, we have to make a fifteen-foot leap, placing ourselves in among the growth. Staying Christian demands the proper perspective.

A word of caution is advised here. To make the leap will have an impact on our attitude toward God the Father, and I would suggest the reader keep that attitude open until at least the finish of chapter 8 of this book. For now, let's see how Jesus' words in verses 1 and 2 apply to us, and what kind of image of the Father they suggest. It is certainly far removed from what we conceived when we pictured ourselves standing beside God on a serene morning. Instead of seeing an amiable gardener humming a tune as he goes about his work over there at the vine, we suddenly wake up to the truth that God is a very exacting Lord with a pruning knife in his hand, heading right for us. He plans to take a long hard look and then cut us off at our lifeline and throw us into the fire, or chop us back so that we can become more productive. It will depend on how he reads what he sees of us as we are suspended mute in his presence.

The image scares people. When I share these thoughts in a Bible class or in a sermon, I am met with horrified stares. Christians are not sure they want to hear these ideas. But when we think about it, that is exactly what Jesus had in mind.

God has a purpose and a mission. He takes that mission seriously, not putting up with a casual or lukewarm dispatching of it. The onus is on us as Christians to carry out that purpose. Jesus is not talking to the world at large in John 15.

He is speaking specifically to his disciples, putting tough standards before us that simply do not apply to those outside the fold. Something extra has always been expected of the Christian. He referred to "Every branch of *mine*. . . . " Though it may not seem quite fair to us, the Lord seems to have a much tougher scale for us than for other people. The perceptive gardener with a pruning knife in hand is not coming at us because we are human. He is coming at us because we are his and he has been counting on us.

When God takes his hard look at each of us, he will discover that either we are bearing fruit or we are not. There are no shades of gray on this one, and no excuses. Either we are or we are not. William Temple once observed, "It is possible to be genuinely drawn to the Lord, to follow His call, to be of His company, and still to bear no fruit."[1] Something went wrong. Something failed to happen. A person religiously puts in the time, carries the name Christian, says the right words, and yet lives a spiritual life that is totally unproductive. We know people like that and grieve for them. They bear no fruit.

In the Upper Room the disciples had firsthand experience to which Jesus may have been alluding. Their dear friend and three-year companion, Judas, had slipped out to put in motion the wheels that would roll to the brow of Golgotha. It was Judas of whom Peter would say a few weeks later, "He was numbered among us, and was allotted his share in this ministry" (Acts 1:17). What happened? Why Judas? He had been a part of the vine. The resources of Jesus were available to him day after day. Though the term "Christian" had not come into play during Jesus' earthly ministry, Judas certainly was what at that time a Christian would appear to be. But he had not borne spiritual fruit and so he was cut off.

Jesus wanted his remaining disciples to know the full truth. Sometimes the cutting-off process is not the voluntary walking-out of a disgruntled member. Sometimes the best way to understand it is to know that God the Father, himself, brought his arm down and cut a person off at the spiritual lifeline. He had scrutinized the branch and saw that it bore no fruit. He saw a lifeless hanger-on, a leech draining the vine's sap and posing a danger to the other branches. In his judgment the condition had gone on long enough and the pruning knife fell. "Every branch of mine that bears no fruit, he takes away."

The spiritual resources needed to bear fruit are available to all Christians. Jesus has given us his life's blood, his essence, that we might be equipped for fruitful lives. At some point God wants to observe his efforts coming to blossom in every branch. Where fruit is not visible, he wants to know why. When the Father sees a Christian who has become a detriment to the vine, His arm is raised. "Every branch of mine that bears no fruit, he takes away."

But what happens if the Lord does see fruit in us? After the harsh-sounding words for those who bore no fruit, those of us who sense we have borne fruit expect good news. A reward would not be out of the question, we think. Having done well, we assume our territory will be expanded, onward and upward, bigger and better, up the rungs of the spiritual ladder to greater successes in the faith.

Again, Jesus has another idea. In fact, he topples our entire philosophy of life. "Every branch of mine that does bear fruit he prunes that it may bear more fruit."

Though that sentence explodes our assumptions, it does put us in closer touch with real-life experience, explaining it for us in a pastoral way. I often find that just at the moment when I think life is going so well, just as I begin to pride myself for all the good works I am doing, I am trimmed or cut back. I don't know about you, but I respond poorly to that. When I am unexpectedly hit with a defeat or setback, I am tempted to say, "What's the use?" or, "Discipleship doesn't make sense." When any person is cut back after doing well, he or she stands on the verge of throwing in the towel, giving it all up as a pointless charade. Or the temptation can take a different flavor.

When a conscientious Christian suffers a setback, even if that Christian has been responsible in obedience to Christ, the setback connotes punishment for wrongdoing. Suffering implies guilt. Occasionally we come across a Christian who gave up on the faith because a particular defeat was interpreted to mean, "God is angry at me. I am unworthy. I do not deserve to be a Christian."

For such a soul, Jesus' harsh and unfair-sounding words in the second half of verse 2 actually provide comfort and inspiration. They provide something for a Christian to grasp when life tumbles in. The radically new thought Jesus offers is simply this: Some setbacks occur in our lives not because we have been naughty; they occur because we have been nice. While Scripture does not give us a blanket explanation of suffering, some hurt comes into our lives for the very reason that we have done what is pleasing in the eyes of God and he sees a way for us to do even better. The pain came for the purpose of helping us grow stronger. God has taken action in our lives to enable us to bear more fruit.

This is never an easy lesson to learn. It certainly wasn't for me. Some years ago I arrived at one of the churches I have been privileged to serve, carrying with me the manuscript of a book on which I had been working for two and one-half years. I had been in consultation with a publishing house, and they liked the idea enough to suggest a few changes that could lead to publication. All the studying had been done and notes filed neatly in a box with all of my two and one-half years of materials and, of course, the manuscript itself. Exhausted from unpacking, I put the box on the carpet beside my desk in the new office and went home for the day. When I entered my office the next morning, there was no box. I searched everywhere and could not find it. Then I had a terrible thought. A quick dash to the rear of the church revealed my worst fears had come to be. The custodian had assumed I meant to throw away the "trash" on the floor. He had carted the box to the incinerator and, thinking he was helping the new minister move in, burned absolutely everything in it. Two and one-half years of hopes, dreams, hard work quite literally went up in smoke and were still smoldering when I gazed into the incinerator. The next Sunday my scheduled sermon topic was "The Wrath of God," a sermon delivered with more than the usual amount of feeling.

Though John 15 did not come to mind at that time, in retrospect it has helped me understand why my loss might have occurred. Yes, I was foolish to put something of value in a container that could be mistaken for trash; and, yes, those things will happen. But I have come firmly to believe that the Lord was telling me something. As a pastor setting out to shepherd a flock, it was not for me to hole up in a study and sharpen a manuscript. My call was to be a pastor to that congregation. One cherished item was taken away that I might concentrate on what the Lord believed to be more important at that time. As I look back I see he was quite right. My ministry has borne more fruit as a result of my losing painfully what could have been a diversion at a crucial time in my ministry. The Lord's pruning knife had been skillfully used.

The Greek word for "pruned" can also be understood to mean "cleansed." This meaning points ahead to our next chapter. It also illustrates how the Lord will strip away from us those things which, in modern vernacular, "mess us up." God strips away aspects of our lives that need to be removed for our spiritual well-being, but which we would not strip away on our own. No one, for example, could have convinced me to burn that manuscript. Some pain comes into our lives when God rips away something to which we have been clinging too tightly. Again in the modern idiom, he helps us "clean up our act."

The writer of the New Testament book of Hebrews drew on the wisdom of Proverbs when he wrote, "Do not regard lightly the discipline of the Lord, nor lose courage when you are punished by him. For the Lord disciplines him whom he loves, and chastises every son whom he receives" (Hebrews 12:5-6; cf. Proverbs 3:11-12).

When it occurs, discipline seems painful. We do not like it nor would we choose it. But later it yields fruit in the lives of those who have been trained by it. Someone said, "God is never closer to us than when he is cutting us back."

T. DeWitt Talmage once wrote,

> A grape vine says, in the early spring, "How glad I am to get through the winter! I shall have no more trouble now! Summer weather will come, and the garden will be very beautiful!" But the gardener comes, and cuts the vine here and there with his knife. The twigs begin to fall, and the grape-vine calls out, "Murder! What are you cutting me for?" "Ah," says the gardener, "I don't mean to kill you. If I did not do this, you would be the laughing-stock of all the other vines before the season is over." Months go on, and one day the gardener comes under the trellis, where the great clusters of grapes hang, and the grape-vine says, "Thank you, sir, you could not have done anything so kind as to have cut me with that knife. . . . " No pruning, no grapes;

no grinding-mill, no flour; no battle, no victory; no cross, no crown![2]

Jesus cared very much what would happen to his disciples across the years. For this reason his words at the outset of John 15 are not soft or comfortable. They are tough and have a bite to them. To stay Christian we need to take them seriously, to view them from the proper perspective. The vine-dresser looks us over with a discerning eye. We are held accountable. He expects each branch to bear fruit.

Notes

[1] William Temple, *Readings in St. John's Gospel* (London: Macmillan, 1940), p. 255.

[2] From a sermon entitled "The Broken Pitchers," quoted in *20 Centuries of Great Preaching,* vol. 5 (Waco, Texas: Word Books, 1971), p. 291.

CHAPTER 3

Already in Your Heart Right Now

"You are already made clean by the word which I have spoken to you" (John 15:3).

I returned from my summer vacation in 1973 with recurrent chest pains. Results would eventually reveal no heart problem, but not before I had been run through an elaborate battery of tests.

I wasn't going to bother too much about it, my hypochondria coming amazingly under control. But my wife insisted that I alert our family physicians to the warning signals I had been receiving. As I had an appointment anyway, I mentioned in as offhanded a manner as I could that I had been having chest pains and my wife seemed concerned.

The next thing I knew, I was stretched out on the table familiar to all doctors' examining rooms. I could see wires running out of a machine to various points on my skin where rubber tips nestled in some kind of goo. I was having an electrocardiogram taken. Out of the machine came a "ticker tape" with lines dancing up and down to the rhythm of my heartbeat. Evidently one of the lines zigged at a point where the doctor thought a zag might have been more appropriate, and I was sent off to see a cardiologist whose office was in the hospital building.

While he could not see the inappropriate zig and thought everything looked quite normal, he did not like the recurrent pain. He suggested that I undergo a diagnostic procedure called a heart catheterization.

My mind flashed back immediately to the hospital visit I had made to a parishioner a few months before. I remembered that when he had described what was involved in having "a cath," as veterans of the procedure call it, I had hoped quietly I would never have to go through that. The man had described how a small tube, or catheter, was to be run up an artery from his right elbow into his heart, and how a dye would then be injected into his heart so that its activity could be monitored.

Hearing that I was a subject for the same test, I realized instantly that I feared the test more than I feared the results. Though I did not know the exact condition of my ticker, I did know it was beating faster than usual as I left the cardiologist's office.

The events of the next stress-filled days still stick vividly in my memory. The image of my children—what they were doing, what they were wearing—at the time I headed for the hospital is crystal clear as though it were only yesterday. Once in the hospital, I was a bundle of nerves. After a night of tossing and turning, I was put on a stretcher to be wheeled away from my room. Many times I had walked the corridors of that hospital and looked down on people being carted past. The view and the feeling were quite different looking up at faces staring down at me. I wanted to hide from their glances. After what seemed an eternity, though it was probably only ten minutes waiting in the hallway, I was rolled into the room where the procedure was to take place. I was put into what looked like an apparatus from an outer-space movie.

As the procedure began, a nurse cleaned the area in the crook of my right arm and deadened it with a few injections of novocaine. I then felt a mild tugging sensation, but no discomfort. The nurse asked if I wanted to watch, and my negative answer must have startled her with its force. I did ask if she would let me know when she started "to run that thing up my arm." I wanted to be braced for that. I wanted to count down to the moment of truth, the surgical invasion. Her voice came back, "Oh, we're already in your heart now." That was an amazing bit of news.

Instantly I was relieved that what I figured would be an excruciating process had already passed unnoticed by me. But just as instantly, I felt embarrassed to have been so worked up over what proved to be so little.

The procedure was far from finished, and of course there were the results to be concerned about. But for me, just knowing that the catheter was in my heart and we were under way lifted a tremendous burden. Now I knew what this complicated procedure felt like. I agreed with Helen Hayes's statement about opening nights: "Everything is worse in anticipation." When the matter-of-fact voice said, "Oh, we're already in your heart now," the fright of anticipation evaporated and I was ready to carry on. The situation had been made new. From that point everything went beautifully.

This experience came to mind as I thought about the transition Jesus made between what was the theme of our last section and the theme of our present verse. As I mentioned in the last chapter, when I talk about God the Father coming at us with a pruning knife in his hand, people shrink back in fear. They wonder when God will act upon them. When will the knife come down to cut us off or cut us back? What will it be like? How will we know it's happening? As with my shuddering prior to the hospital procedure, Christians quake at the thought of God taking such definite action in their lives. Happily, Helen Hayes can turn theologian on this one. Being pruned may well be worse in anticipation.

To ease his disciples' fright, Jesus offered reassuring words immediately on the heels of his teaching about being pruned. John 15:3 reads: "You are already made clean by the word which I have spoken to you." The English translation might make us miss what Jesus was trying to do. Being pruned and being cleaned would seem to have nothing in common in our language. However, a word study of the original biblical tongue reveals that Jesus deliberately used rather awkward construction to build a bridge between pruning and cleaning. Verse 3 is a comment on verse 2. A loose paraphrase of the passage might go something like this: "Yes, the vinedresser is coming at you to render his verdict and cut you back; but realize much of the work has already been done." Jesus did not want his disciples paralyzed by fright in anticipation, fretting over what might be. He wanted them to build confidence on what had already occurred.

The confidence he sought was not an arrogance at what the disciples had accomplished. Rather it was to be an assurance that God was already accomplishing his purpose in their lives. The focus remains on God, as Christians discover the foundation on which to build spiritual stamina. Jesus was calling the disciples outside themselves, to remember what had been done to them by One other than themselves. Just as a branch cannot prune itself but must be pruned, so the disciples could not make themselves clean but had to be made clean. This, Jesus declared, had already been done, with God using as his instrument the Word which he had uttered.

When John was on the Isle of Patmos some years later, he had a vision of the risen Christ, and " . . . from his mouth issued a sharp two-edged sword" (Revelation 1:16). Perhaps on Patmos he recalled what Jesus had said in the Upper Room, and remembered how the Lord's word always has a cutting edge. Perhaps he thought of his own life and how like a pruning knife the word had pruned him, making him clean.

Manford George Gutske wrote:

> . . . the Scriptures are useful in pruning. Reading and thoughtful studying of the Bible will actually have the effect of cleansing out some things in the life of a Christian which are not in accord with the will of God. This is a necessary and natural process in growth. Many habits and ways, some of which may not be evil in themselves nor harmful in other persons, are not fruitful and do not help toward Christian character. God wants these to be cut out.[1]

The tense of the verb in John 15:3 offers the consoling truth that some of the cutting has already occurred.

John 15:3 leaves us with two bits of advice on how to stay Christian. They stand as two sides of the same coin.

1. Though the Word has already been spoken, and has already acted upon us, we need constantly to hear it anew, and continually live under its discipline.

I have long been haunted by the parable of the rich man and Lazarus. You recall the story. The rich man was surrounded on earth by splendor, while Lazarus was doomed to be a beggar at the rich man's gate. In eternity the roles were reversed. Lazarus wound up in heaven with Father Abraham, while the rich man sweltered in the agony of Hades. Calling up from his misery, the rich man pleaded with Father Abraham, begging to have Lazarus sent back to earth. The rich man wanted a warning delivered to his five brothers so that they would know the truth about how to live their lives and the truth about eternal judgment. But Abraham coldly refused the request. His reasoning was that the trip would be both unnecessary and futile. "They have Moses and the prophets; let them hear them" (Luke 16:29). The Word of God has already been put to them. If they refuse to let the Word act in their lives, that will be their problem. No further message need be sent. They have already been told.

The writer to the Hebrews declared that " . . . good news came to us just as to them; but the message which they heard did not benefit them, because it did not meet with faith in the hearers" (Hebrews 4:2).

God's initiative expects our follow-through in response. If I might coin a term, discipleship calls for "response-ability," the ability to respond. Some people seem unable to do it. They are fantastic at causing things to happen, initiating, manipulating, controlling. But they cannot humble themselves and respond in thanksgiving to what has already been done on their behalf. Ten lepers were healed by Jesus, but only one had "response-ability" enough to come back in gratitude (Luke 17:11-19).

Charles Eerdman put forth a challenge to all Christians. "The disciples, who had received this word, were cleansed, in principle, and potentially; but in experience every follower of Christ must apply to his own life this pruning knife, if fruit is to be produced in character and service."[2] Though we cannot ultimately prune ourselves, we can cooperate and participate in what God is doing. We can respond. Let the Word act in your life.

2. We can build our assurance on the "already." This is extremely important for a Christian because life in Christ re-

quires a proper balance between the already and the not yet. Jesus could say, "You are already made clean," while knowing sins continue within us and we are not yet what we are meant to be. As Colleen Townsend Evans wrote, "The truth is that I don't know of anyone who has been 'made clean' totally. We are all in process at one point or another."[3]

The question for us Christians is where to place our emphasis. Charles Swindoll has recently published a book on persevering through pressure. He wrote to help Christians "hang in there." One of his chapters is entitled "Inferiority: Contagious Plague of Self-Doubt." In it he writes, "The one who frequently feels inferior is the one who concentrates on the part that isn't finished rather than on the part that is being completed or has already been shaped."[4]

Growth in Christ often involves a longing for deeper experience or something more in our faith. We want to be fully what Christ intends and we know we haven't arrived. Though we hang on our walls the adage "Have patience, God isn't finished with me yet," and hope other people will read it, the fact is that we often don't heed our own slogans. We lose patience with ourselves, unfinished products that we are. When we see a Christian a bit further along in the spiritual journey, we fall into a tailspin. "Why can't I be like that?" we wonder. "What is wrong with me?"

Jesus told his disciples and he tells us that we have already been made clean. Of course there is more to come. But something has already happened in your life and in mine. Don't underestimate God's care in providing us all we need at our present stage of spiritual growth. To stay Christian, focus on what the Lord has done. Build on the experience he has chosen to give you. Something has already happened or you would not be a Christian. Build on it. Accentuate the already.

The theme of this chapter has been overcoming the debilitating worry over what we anticipate—the not yet. It is overcome for us in the same way my fright over my heart catheterization was overcome—when I realized the already. Jesus followed his ominous words in verse 2 with reassuring words in verse 3. Loosely paraphrased, it reads: "Don't worry about what is yet to be. By the power of my word, I am already in your heart right now."

Notes

[1]Manford George Gutzke, *Plain Talk on John* (Grand Rapids, Mich.: The Zondervan Corp., 1968), p. 154.

[2]Charles Eerdman, *The Gospel of John* (Philadelphia: The Westminster Press, 1916), p. 133.

[3]Colleen Townsend Evans, *The Vine Life* (Lincoln, Va.: Chosen Books, 1980), p. 50.

[4]Charles R. Swindoll, *Three Steps Forward, Two Steps Back* (Nashville: Thomas Nelson Inc., 1980), p. 130.

Abide

"Abide in me, and I in you" (John 15:4).

One week, early in my ministry, I panicked. The worst thing that could ever happen to a preacher was happening to me. With Sunday rapidly approaching, I had run out of things to say. I could just imagine the congregation perched on their pews, anticipating about twenty minutes of well-prepared preaching. But as I stared blankly at the sheet of paper in my typewriter that Thursday afternoon, it dawned on me that I had about four minutes to give them if I read everything I had, slowly . . . twice. While I have never known a congregation to complain about a sermon being too short, I suspected that unless something happened quickly, my preaching career was in its late innings.

I am sure one of the primary ways the Lord keeps us preachers close to him is by reminding us of our complete dependence on him. I marvel at how he provides for me week after week, often quite miraculously. He certainly did that particular week, giving me not only a sermon, but a very crucial insight as well.

I had assumed that the most important part in preparing a sermon was "cranking it out." As a result I would spend hours going over the outline, going over every sentence, making sure every word was just so. Then I would practice the delivery, memorizing every little inflection. This was an excellent discipline and one that ought to be followed in some degree by every young pulpit aspirant.

What I learned that week, however, which turned my ministry around, was that the Lord wanted more. He wanted me to know that "cranking out" a sermon, while always extremely important, can never become what my faith, my ministry, or even my preaching is all about. Any Christian who concentrates exclusively on putting out will eventually dry up. If all we do is put out, we will soon run out. I had been spending so much time honing my sermons that I had cut back on my study and devotion time. The Lord was hearing from me in the professional capacity of "the Reverend," but he was not hearing enough from just plain John.

If we want to be productive in God's kingdom, we need to realize that he has a rhythm for our lives and he expects us to flow with it. Rather than concentrating simply on meeting all the demands of producing, we are called to be "supply-sided" in our spiritual economy. That is, God realizes that before we can bear fruit, we ourselves need to take nourishment. Before we can put out, we need to take in. If we want to bear fruit, we must first abide. What an odd twist that being productive in God's mission comes only when we make production a secondary concern which ranks behind our receiving from him. Bearing fruit is a function of abiding. "As the branch cannot bear fruit by itself, unless it abides in the vine, neither can you, unless you abide in me" (John 15:4). "Abide in me."

The key that unlocks the early verses of John 15 is the word "abide." So central is it to Jesus' theme, that he drops the word into his conversation ten times in seven verses. To illustrate what this word meant, Jesus offered his analogy of the vine and its branches. Abiding means that we are to Christ as a branch is to its vine.

There is no reason to believe Jesus had any cryptic code in this analogy. His urgent teaching was offered in a straight-from-the-shoulder basic way, using an analogy to be understood at its simplest, most obvious level. For example, a quick glance out of my study window will instantly show me what I already knew: all the living branches I can see are structurally attached to a vine or a trunk. The disciples would know that "abiding" implied *being connected to Jesus.*

Several persons have referred to "cut-flower Christians" who are just like the cut flowers we arrange and put on the credenza. They have a prominent place for a time and adorn the room with beauty. They would seem to be the envy of the flower kingdom. But they are cut flowers. No matter how much water we put in the vase to keep them going, they are cut off from their real source of life and soon will wither and die.

I believe that when Jesus used the word "abide" in the sense of being connected to him, he had in mind our participation in his church. Paul referred to the Christian congregation as "the Body of Christ." If we want to know ourselves as connected to Christ, we need to be connected to the church which is his body. Theodore Parker Ferris once wrote that "a person can live a good life outside the church but he cannot live a Christian life outside the church, for there is no Christianity without the Christian community."[1] Staying Christian will involve a higher view of the church than many persons, even church members, may suppose.

In an excellent study of John's Gospel, Father Raymond Brown writes that the Greek word for "falling away" comes from the root which led to our words "scandal" and "scandalize." " 'Scandal' is what trips up a disciple and takes him from Jesus' company; or [it] is what causes one to give up the true Christian faith and withdraw from the community."[2] Staying Christian is in no small part defined by this insight. Loss of faith does not so much mean an individualized feeling of doubt or internal depression, as it means being cut off from "the company" which is the church. To be a Christian is to be a part of the body, the fellowship, the company of believers.

We can step a rung deeper and say that Jesus intended that we attend worship regularly. One of the major mistakes I made early in my ministry, while serving on a church staff, was to schedule myself out of Sunday morning worship. We had two services, with Sunday church school during both. Wanting to reach as many persons as possible with an important class, I scheduled the class to run during both services to accommodate the varied routines of the parishioners. I kept my nose to the grindstone for three months, missing worship every Sunday morning, while busily working in another part of the church building. Before long I felt myself cut off from the lifeblood of the church. I began to feel like an outsider, not fully a part of what was going on at the church—and I was one of the ministers! I have often reflected on how estranged laypersons must feel from their congregations when they regularly absent themselves from worship.

At the height of worship and the deepest way Jesus wants us to be connected to him, is the celebration of the Lord's Supper. Many denominations, my own Presbyterian church included, have had on their books a rule that any person who misses Communion for a certain period of time has cut himself or herself off from the fellowship, and official action is required. Some Bible commentators go so far as to suggest the analogy of the vine and the branches is to be understood almost solely as a parable of the Eucharist. After all, they argue, John 15 is an excerpt from Jesus' teaching during the first Communion service. The disciples might well have seen the image of a vine and branches, the teaching about abiding, as having to do with the bread and the cup they shared that night. Earlier in his ministry, Jesus had said to them, "Truly, truly, I say to you, unless you eat the flesh of the Son of man and drink his blood, you have no life in you; he who eats my flesh and drinks my blood has eternal life, and I will raise him up at the last day. For my flesh is food indeed and my blood is drink indeed. He who eats my flesh and drinks my blood abides in me, and I in him" (John 6:53-56). Whether a eucharistic interpretation of John 15 is the best one, I do not know. But we cannot mistake the fact that Jesus wants us to be connected to him through his church, at worship and celebrating the sacrament. That is the primary context for feeding.

We also see another important point to Jesus' teaching. *To abide, as a branch, means constancy. It means staying connected for a long period of time.* The church where I was pastor has a clear glass window at the back of the chancel so that every Sunday morning worshipers are able to see the trees outside. As a church we can watch the seasons come and go as the leaves turn amber and fall; then, in time, the limbs sprout buds and fresh green leaves again.

Every week when the congregation files into the sanctuary, the same limbs are attached in the same way to the same trunks outside the chancel window. From week to week the makeup of the worshiping congregation changes. New people arrive. Members travel, or are ill, or move away. But the limbs are there, attached, every week. Even preachers come and go. I take vacations. Guest ministers pinch-hit. But the limbs are still attached. Jesus gave us a challenging image of endurance.

In the early years of this century, the great preacher John Henry Jowett once observed that Jesus deliberately used the word "abide" as a warning against a spasmodic religious life. He was countering the notion that we can drop in on church when we need it or when Grandma comes to visit; otherwise, we can stay home nursing a second cup of coffee and reading the *Sunday Times*. Jesus was saying that church attendance is not to be occasional. Being Christian is a week-after-week lifetime sort of thing. "Let us consider how to stir up one another to love and good works, not neglecting to meet together, as is the habit of some, but encouraging one another, and all the more as you see the Day drawing near" (Hebrews 10:24-25).

If I were asked to give an off-the-cuff definition of the word "abide," I would settle on the word "stay." When a person abides in a particular place, the person is staying there. It becomes home. In part, staying Christian requires a willful decision by us to stay with the Christian community over time, a very long time.

In an excellent study of John's Gospel, Earl Palmer points out that the word "abide" comes from the same root in Greek as a word which appears in the well-known section at the beginning of John 14. In the King James Version it is translated "mansions": "In my Father's house are many mansions" (John 14:2). The Revised Standard Version has "rooms," and Palmer translates it "dwelling places."[3] The point is that the root of the word "abide" has an eternal connotation to it in

Jesus' mind. When we are connected to him, he intends that it last. Like love, abiding endures forever.

Our powers of observation tell us something else about Jesus' analogy. Haven't you seen a limb that has been structurally connected to a live tree for many years and the limb is dead? Structural attachment, and putting in the time, are important prerequisites, but they are not the major course.

A branch is alive and fruitful when the essence of the vine is flowing into it. If the life's essence of the vine is not flowing into the branch, the branch is dead or, as in the case of a cut flower, dying. The branch takes its life, its identity, even bears its fruit from the vine sap.

This means something very specific for our relationship to Christ. Most of us conceive of ourselves as being *with* Christ. But John 15 invites us to a deeper conception of the relationship. Instead of simply being *with* him, we are challenged to know ourselves as being *from* him. Something of his life, his presence, his personality, his power, the very essence of who he is, surges into us, just as the very essence of a vine surges into the branch. Thus Paul, who was no dead branch himself, could write, "It is no longer I who live, but Christ who lives in me" (Galatians 2:20). "We have the mind of Christ" (1 Corinthians 2:16). "For me to live is Christ" (Philippians 1:21). Paul knew himself as a branch shooting out from Christ. Jesus wanted His disciples to know that any Christian can feel the same way. But how? How can we know ourselves as being *from* Christ?

Jesus stretched his analogy a bit at this point. Though no branch ever wills to be attached to a vine, Jesus called for Christians to take willful action. The word "abide" is in the imperative. The Lord evidently expected his disciples to take responsibility, to do those things that would more freely allow his personality to flow into them. *To obey the command to abide (and it is a command) means that Jesus expected them and us to have an attitude of openness, receptivity, readiness, and willingness. In short: Let Christ happen through you.*

The *Scofield Reference Bible* gives a slant on the word "abide."

> To abide in Christ is, on the one hand, to have no sin unjudged and unconfessed, no interest into which He is not brought, no

> life which He cannot share. On the other hand, the abiding one takes all burdens to Him, and draws all wisdom, life and strength from Him. . . . nothing is allowed in the life which separates from Him.[4]

Dr. David Livingstone, who so totally gave his life in service to Christ on the mission field, had a favorite prayer which ought to be etched on the heart of every Christian. "Send me anywhere, only go with me. Lay any burden upon me, only sustain me. Sever any tie that binds but the tie that binds me to Thy service and to Thy heart." Livingstone was a man whose life flowed from Christ, and he bore Christlike fruit.

Staying Christian means maintaining an openness, receptivity, readiness, and willingness for what Christ wills to do through us. It means allowing his purpose to be accomplished through us, as the purpose of a vine is accomplished through a branch. It means that when he says to us, "Follow me," we do it, no matter what that may mean or where it may lead. One commentator said that the verb "to abide" means "walking in the will of God."[5] Another wrote of the disciples' abiding, "Their will must cooperate with His will."[6]

Now we are on the edge of the conclusion, the deepest reaches of Jesus' analogy. *Abiding means letting the will of God be expressed through our lives.* Our conclusion will bring us full circle because it will test how well we are connected to Christ. It will test whether we acknowledge him over time as the true vine that feeds our lives or whether we are really drawing our support elsewhere.

As a pastor I often have people approach me for guidance on what to do. People wonder what God's will is for their lives. For most Christians the dilemma arises not at the point of obeying God's will; the dilemma hits at the point of knowing what that will is in the first place. I have discovered that in part the problem stems from the modern ignorance of the Bible. In Scripture the Lord has taught us what to do but too many people simply have not taken the time to study it. They hope to put their lives together without reading the instruction manual that goes with it. Bible study would make the will of God clearer for many Christians.

But even the Bible points beyond itself to something more. Scripture is never meant to be an exhaustive legal document.

At times its teaching is clear and sufficient; at other times it only suggests or nudges; at still other points it is silent.

In the book of Proverbs we find a passage where Scripture moves into our lives and calls us to attention. "In all thy ways acknowledge him, and he shall direct thy paths" (Proverbs 3:6, KJV). The passage teaches that if we want the Lord to direct our paths—to show us his will—we must first acknowledge him in all our ways. We might say: Be open, receptive, ready, and willing. A person who cannot figure out God's will may be a person who has not taken that first mandatory step of acknowledging him as Lord of everything.

Let me illustrate this point. Suppose John Q. Churchman has a tough decision that he must make and he cannot decide what to do. No novice at decision making, Churchman applies his well-studied techniques. He weighs the alternatives. He may have some utilitarian philosophy in his bones which makes him search for the greatest good for the greatest number. Or, in this psychological era, he may try to get in touch with his inner feelings. He will probably consult friends or history (how have people made the decision in the past and with what results?); or he may look up a few experts for their opinions. And, yes, of course Churchman is a religious man who will consult the Deity.

When he calls the Lord in for consultation, the conversation may go something like this: "Lord, I've got a doozy of a problem. What would you think I ought to do as a Christian on this one?"

The Lord replies."Why do you want to know my will? What difference will it make to you? If I tell you my will, will you do it?"

Churchman flinches. "Let's not get carried away, Lord. Let's not sign any papers up front on this one. Lord, you have to realize how complex life is. You need to remember all the pressure I've been under. And besides, how do I know how the situation might change tomorrow? So let's not tie me down to any promises or commitments. Just let me know what you think I ought to do, and I'll sign off."

The Lord hears quite clearly what Churchman is saying. Churchman wants the Lord of the universe to be one consultant among many. The Lord replies, "Either you will hear me as the Lord of your life, or you will not hear me at all. Either you will stand ready and willing to obey my will, or I will leave you ignorant."

One day many months later, Churchman will pass his pastor on the street and comment how hard it is to know the will of God these days.

Michel Quoist would probably have a helpful comeback to Mr. Churchman. A French priest, Quoist has penned devotional books which reveal him to be a man of unusual spiritual sensitivity. He wrote these words which speak to our theme:

> Son, I want more for you and for the world.
> Until now you have planned your actions, but I have no need of them.
> You have asked for my approval, you have asked for my support,
> You have wanted to interest me in your work.
> But don't you see, Son, that you were reversing the roles?
> I have watched you, I have seen your good will,
> And I want more than you, now.
> You will no longer do your own works, but the will of your Father in heaven.[7]

On that traumatic day when I realized I had run out of things to say, the Lord had a message for me. "Stop slaving over *your* sermons and start offering *mine*." He was reminding me to start acting like a branch. It makes all the difference in the world when we let the life of Christ happen through us. Lo and behold, we see his fruit in our lives!

Notes

[1] *The Interpreter's Bible*, vol. 9, Exposition by Theodore Parker Ferris (Nashville: Abingdon Press, 1959), p. 222.

[2] Raymond E. Brown, S.S., trans., *The Gospel According to John XIII-XXI* (New York: Doubleday & Co. Inc., 1970), p. 690.

[3] Earl F. Palmer, *The Intimate Gospel* (Waco, Tex.: Word Books, 1978), p. 122.

[4] C. I. Scofield, *Holy Bible, Scofield Reference Bible* (New York: Oxford University Press, 1909, 1945), pp. 1136-1137.

[5] Manford Gutzke, *Plain Talk on John* (Grand Rapids, Mich.: The Zondervan Corp., 1968), p. 153.

[6]B. F. Westcott, *The Gospel According to St. John* (Grand Rapids, Mich.: Wm. B. Eerdmans Publishing Co., 1950), p. 217.

[7]Michel Quoist, *Prayers* (New York: Sheed and Ward, Inc., 1963), pp. 122-123. Reprinted with permission of Andrews, McMeel, and Parker.

CHAPTER 5

Bearing Fruit

> "Abide in me, and I in you. As the branch cannot bear fruit by itself, unless it abides in the vine, neither can you, unless you abide in me" (John 15:4).

We come now to the all-important matter of bearing fruit. I must admit that I began my study of John 15 believing that to bear fruit was the ultimate work we were supposed to accomplish, the crowning result of our effort. I dug into commentaries, hoping for step-by-step instructions on how to obey what I had thought was Christ's demand for output. Since bearing fruit was obviously so central to Jesus' teaching, it had to be a command which he would explain how to obey. However, biblical study, like most fields of honest inquiry, sometimes uncovers an unexpected find.

Opening the doors of John 15, I was twice stunned by what I saw within. Two facts about Jesus' use of the term "bearing fruit" literally blew away my assumptions. Only after much further prayer and reflection have I come to appreciate how the dashing of my presuppositions has moved me closer to the central theme of John 15 and how to stay Christian: The

Lord, and not you or I, is the main actor in this drama.

My first dizzying surprise came when, after realizing that the verb "to abide" was in the imperative, I turned to the concept of bearing fruit and discovered it was not an imperative. I was incredulous! Fruit was unmistakably the purpose of abiding in Christ. Fruit would prove we were disciples and bring glory to God. But it was not imperative that you and I bear fruit. Yes, in a few verses Jesus would say that his command was for us to love one another, and yes, love, as we shall see, is a leading mark of a fruitful life. But bearing fruit is not in itself a command. Amazing!

Some readers might argue that I am nitpicking. They could claim that Jesus did not need to command anyone to bear fruit. His disciples would readily infer from all that was said about fruit that Christians were expected to produce it.

I have concluded, however, that Jesus chose his words carefully for directness, not inference, in his farewell discourse. When he wanted to lay down a law, he laid it down. He used the imperative when he wanted it, and did not employ the imperative when he did not want it. I believe he deliberately avoided making a command of fruit-bearing and did so for a reason.

Henri Nouwen has written that " . . . like all great disciples of Jesus, Mother Teresa affirmed again the truth that ministry can be fruitful only if it grows out of a direct and intimate encounter with our Lord."[1] Therein lies the key. Fruit grows out of something else. Commands are something that can be obeyed or disobeyed directly. They do not pertain to by-products. In the rhythm of life in Christ, we are commanded to abide in him so that fruit will happen as a by-product. Throughout the early verses of John 15, fruit is repeatedly portrayed as a function of abiding. When we abide, we are fruitful. ("He who abides in me, and I in him, he it is that bears much fruit," v. 5). When we do not abide, we cannot bear fruit. ("As the branch cannot bear fruit by itself, unless it abides in the vine, neither can you, unless you abide in me," v. 4). Fruit happens or fails to happen, depending upon whether we obey the command to abide. As a result, bearing fruit could not be set apart as a separate mandate.

Just as I was reeling from the jolt of discovering that fruit-bearing is not a command, I was belted again. This time the punch came from realizing that John 15 would give me no clear-cut working definition of fruit-bearing and I might as well quit looking for one. Frankly, I almost quit everything. Wanting to share with my fellow disciples how to stay Christian, I wanted something worth putting before them, particularly on a subject so pivotal to all of us as bearing fruit. After I had preached on the text in verse 2 about how every branch would be pruned, several people approached me with a common request. "Let me know when you plan to preach on bearing fruit. I don't want to miss that one. I hope you will tell us just what bearing fruit is all about." Imagine my disappointment when I realized that biblical integrity prevented me from offering them what they sought. But then biblical integrity often does that to preachers.

I empathized with the congregation wanting to know exactly what bearing fruit meant. After all, if God is going to assess my life according to whether I bear fruit, you had better believe I want a precise definition of bearing fruit. If I am expected to measure up to a rigorous standard, I don't think it is too much to ask that I be told exactly what that standard is. If bearing fruit will prove that I am a disciple, I want to know when I am on target. What does bearing fruit mean? When parishioners told me they were looking forward to the message on fruit-bearing, I responded honestly, "And so am I." What I did not say was that my research to that point had me worried. Subsequent prayer and study merely made matters worse. Bearing fruit was not to be defined.

Jesus very wisely and, I believe, very deliberately kept his language vague. And that very vagueness is a reminder to all disciples that fruit-bearing is not our work but his. By staying undefined, this passage of Scripture stays free from abuse. Let's face it; a specific definition from Jesus would quickly degenerate into little more than a means for overly zealous disciples to show their worth. A precise measurement of fruit-bearing would provide our competitive instincts all that would be needed to start racking up points on an imaginary, or not so imaginary, scoreboard. I once heard a teenager comment after a youth rally, "I got four conversions this week, but Sally only got two." I cannot conceive of Jesus wanting such antics to occur. Nor can I possibly imagine that he is anything but hurt by it. The very thought of a scoreboard is diametrically opposed to his personality, method, and teaching. How wise he was to keep it vague.

When it finally sank in that Jesus does not want me to know what fruit-bearing is, I could not escape the obvious implication. My tacit definition of bearing fruit had either to be dropped or stilled. I faced a moment of truth that was both difficult and controversial. Winning souls to Jesus Christ, which I had assumed was *the* definition of fruit-bearing, could no longer be called *the* definition because no clear definition exists. This truth is difficult because I know Jesus elsewhere teaches that we are to make disciples of all nations (Matthew 28:19). Scripture looks forward to the day when "at the name of Jesus Christ every knee should bow . . . and every tongue confess that Jesus Christ is Lord . . . " (Philippians 2:10-11). It is controversial because any attempt to mute the work of winning souls to Jesus Christ sounds like the devil's doing.

How then does John 15 teach truth about fruit-bearing without undermining Christian evangelism? My study of John 15 reveals that, by preventing soul-winning from being *the* definition of fruit-bearing, we actually are freed to embrace what Christian evangelism is meant to be.

Someone put a finger on a basic insight. "It is not the work of the branch to engraft another branch onto the vine. The vine will produce other branches." We are branches. It is for us simply to bear fruit. Winning converts is not our primary reason for being. If we make it primary, we run the risk of trying to play God, which inevitably invites trouble.

We will begin to believe that our worth is measured by what happens in someone else's life. Simply put, I will measure *my* discipleship in terms of whether *he* or *she* is converted. That is totally unbiblical and grotesquely unfair to me and to the other person. We will get down on ourselves when persons close to us are not converted as a result of their proximity to us and what we had hoped was our contagious faith. Of course we are hurt by their lack of faith. But that is not the same thing as condemning ourselves. I have seen parents drop away from the church because they became convinced their faith was impotent. Perhaps one of their children has strayed into some far country away from Christianity. Since Mom and Dad are convinced that they are commanded to convert their offspring, they have no alternative logically but to see themselves as disobedient failures. If they could only realize that bearing fruit is not so neatly defined in terms of soul-winning, this false sense of guilt would diminish and they would be freer to relate to their children in Christian love. Mark it down in your book of thoughts to live by: The validity of your faith is not dependent on what happens in someone else's life.

The fact remains, however, that I do feel down when those around me are untouched by my witnessing; and I feel fulfilled when I see people growing in or into the faith at the same time I am praying for them or ministering to them in some way. Let's face it: As Christians we want to reach people for Christ.

Jesus' teaching recorded in John 15 does not deny us that. What our Lord wanted to stress was that you and I can do more for persons we want to reach when we realize that the life-changing act of "converting" them is not our job. Persons can be converted only by the movement of the Holy Spirit. It is the Lord's work. It is for me prayerfully and faithfully and lovingly only to set the stage. Maybe this is why the Bible calls us witnesses and not soul-winners.

A story is told about Dwight L. Moody. He was walking along a Chicago street one afternoon when he came upon a drunk passed out in the gutter. From the other side of the street a mocking voice cried out, "Hey, Moody, is that one of your converts?" To this the noted evangelist had a quick reply, "He probably *is* one of *my* converts. A convert of the *Holy Spirit* would never behave this way." Moody well knew that when we mortals try to play God, the results are usually disastrous.

The apostle Paul shared this belief. To the Corinthians he wrote, "I planted, Apollos watered, and God gave the growth" (1 Corinthians 3:6). Paul never was one to be wholly passive. He and Apollos took initiative and had a hand in it. One planted; the other watered. But it was God who gave the growth.

Think of the spouse (for the sake of discussion, let's say it was the wife) who has been attending a prayer group for some time. One day the Lord moves and she senses the grace of

Jesus Christ flowing over her as never before. Her life is bursting at the seams with a joy which she wants to share with everyone, even if she must be a bit silly or giddy about doing it. While this is a happy time for her, it is also dangerous. Not only is her faith experiencing the vulnerability and dependency of a spiritual infant, but her family could be on the verge of an onslaught by an overly zealous spokesperson for Jesus.

Her husband and children will not miss the fact that something is different about Mom. She has not bounced and bubbled around the house this way before. She will probably tell of what happened, unfortunately adding a wrinkle that undermines the whole thing. Wanting to share how she had felt herself spiritually dead in comparison to what she now feels, she will give the impression that a person is spiritually lifeless unless that person has had an experience just like the one she has had at the prayer group. Add to this message the expressed hope that her husband will have the same thing happen to him that happened to her, and you have trouble. While she is joyfully announcing that she will be praying for him, he is becoming hostile and she cannot figure out why.

The answer is clear. She put him in the impossible situation of either reenacting *her* experience or being made to feel spiritually inadequate because he has not had it. She has not given the Holy Spirit room to permit her husband to have the kind of experience that the Spirit has in store uniquely for him. Her husband's hostility stems from his desire to have his own experience with the Spirit which her overly zealous pushings prevent him from having.

Bearing fruit is not primarily to be understood as winning converts to Jesus, admirable as that may sound. Jesus wants fruit-bearing to be vague so that we will not be too pushy and manipulative, actually getting in the Lord's way.

All of this sounds quite negative to me as I reread what has been written. So far in this chapter I have spent quite a bit of time discussing what bearing fruit is not. But what shall I do? My study of John 15 has convinced me that the contemporary church needs to hear this negative message lest it take off at cross purposes to Jesus' teaching. So I do not intend to erase what I have written. Rather I choose to move on. The problem to be faced now is what to do with our desire to reach other people for Christ, if soul-winning is not *the* definition of fruit-bearing.

The answer comes as we fall back on Jesus' simple yet profound analogy of the vine and the branches. While a strict definition is impossible, the analogy hints at a few general directions. *A branch is acknowledged to be fruit-bearing if it is making fruit available.* When an apple tree has borne apples, it has made food available. I have never seen a branch laden with apples leap down to the ground and begin chasing around the community shaking apples on people's front lawns. The apple tree branch does not ring door bells and insist residents bite into apples right on the spot. All I have ever seen an apple tree, or any vine and branches, do is make food available. It is expected to do no less, and certainly no more.

A seminary professor gave preachers a bit of sound advice when he wrote that "it is not the duty of ministers of the Word to convert; it is only their duty prayerfully to preach the Word. Less than this they ought not to do; more they cannot do."[2] Preachers are like all Christians on this one. Our calling is to make the Word available. Tell the story—put the word out—make sure it is available. But then give it room. Let the Holy Spirit in on it.

In Bible study groups I have often used the example of what I call "casserole evangelism." Most church groups are familiar with the tremendous service and ministry that comes to families at a time of crisis, when food is brought to the home. Now can you imagine how preposterous it would be for a deaconess to take a piping hot casserole to the door and demand that the family wolf it down right before her eyes? How rude it would be for a church worker to expect proof that the casserole was eaten at all! When we take food to a family's door, we really have no idea whether they will eat it soon after we leave, or whether they will share it with others, or whether they will cram it down the disposal. Though of course we are interested, that really is not our business. We sensed a need and we made food available. What happens to it after that is, as it should be, out of our control.

Evangelism is meant to be that way. We cannot force people to consume the gospel. We engage in the ludicrous when we demand early signs that a person has taken in and digested what we are pushing on him. All we can do is make spiritual nourishment available . . . no more and no less.

Second, we bear fruit when we reach out to meet human needs. While communicating the Word in words of our own is mandatory (and I have dedicated my life to doing just that), I need to be reminded, along with all Christians, of one simple fact. Fruit is silent. The bearing of fruit that Jesus had in mind involves body language. Tell the Good News, but always remember that sometimes actions do speak louder than words. When the disciples gathered in the Upper Room, Jesus set the tone of the evening by stooping down and washing the disciples' feet. Over the protest of some, he dramatically illustrated who he was, this vine whose fruit they were to bear.

Elton Trueblood put our chapters on "abiding" and "bearing fruit" in a proper light when he wrote, "Service without devotion is rootless; devotion without service is fruitless."[3]

Some commentators believe that Jesus took his image of the vine and branches from the Old Testament, in which Israel is often compared to a vine. By saying, "I am the *true* vine," Jesus picked up on the fact that the Old Testament vine was generally described as a disobedient failure. Isaiah 5 is a chapter we have come to know as "The Song of the Vineyard." The vineyard is condemned to doom because the society it represents has been given over to exploitation, injustice, drunkenness, idolatry, and a warped sense of values. The Lord repeatedly calls for social responsibility and, like the gardener with a pruning knife in his hand, holds us accountable for our social behavior.

Ray Stedman tells of a man who opened a resort which he dedicated to the Lord. He combed the country to find thirty college students who would qualify to work with him for a summer. He interviewed well over three hundred applicants to find the right thirty. Each applicant was asked three questions: "Do you love work? Do you love people? Do you love Jesus?" Only those who wholeheartedly said yes to all three could meet the requirements of the job.

As guests arrived, these dedicated young people would work feverishly to give each person the most enjoyable time of his or her life. After about three or four days, guests would seek out the resort owner to inquire where he found such wonderful young people. He would then reveal his three questions. When the guests raised their eyebrows about asking if the students loved Jesus, the owner responded that he knew the workers could not keep up with the rigors of caring for the guests if they did not love Jesus.

That was it. The resort had no Bible studies, no prayer meetings. Indeed, it was for all intents and purposes secular. But before long the guests began to sense their own lives being changed. Because these young disciples loved Jesus and served people, conversions just happened as a by-product.[4]

In *The Cross and the Switchblade*, Dave Wilkerson described how he would send young people into the streets of New York to do evangelistic work. "They would go not with an eye to gaining converts but with an eye to meeting need."[5]

If we are genuinely reaching out to meet the needs of another person, we are bearing fruit. Even if that person continues for a long time to appear absolutely turned off by Christianity, our acts of love are the fruit Jesus wants to see.

We make nourishment available; we meet human need; and finally *we bear fruit simply by being a person in Jesus Christ*. When Christ's Holy Spirit lives in our lives, certain qualities (interestingly enough called fruits of the Spirit) become evident. Paul lists what a Christian can expect to be. "But the fruit of the Spirit is love, joy, peace, patience, kindness, goodness, faithfulness, gentleness, self-control" (Galatians 5:22-23). A person who lives these qualities is a fruit-bearing personality.

I like the story told of George Whitefield. The noted evangelist had just concluded a service when someone approached him with a nosy question. "Mr. Whitefield, do you see that man over there? Is he a Christian?" The gifted preacher might have tried to get information about the man's church attendance, or his prayer life, or whether he had made a public profession of faith. But he skipped religion for the moment and said simply, "I do not know. I haven't talked to his wife." She would know, wouldn't she? His wife would have the secret of knowing what kind of person he really was. Whitefield gauged a person's faith by the quality of his personal life.

In my years of ministry one woman stands out in my memory for the way she faced an extended terminal illness and eventually a painful death. There are many reasons why I might have dreaded calling on her. But I did not. In fact I rather looked forward to visiting her, not because I enjoy seeing people who are in pain or because I relish having a chance to be pastoral when a person needs help. I looked forward to my visits with this gracious woman because she exuded love, joy, and peace. In our encounters I do not know if I helped her or not, but I do know that she ministered to me. She was a Christian whose life bore fruit. I know it. She had to be bearing fruit because I came away from every meeting with her knowing I had been fed.

Until midway through my college years, our family spent every summer on a farm in Falls Village, Connecticut, a small town tucked in the northwest corner of the state. I remember a pear tree that stood off to one side, down a hill behind the house. While I was growing up I was not particularly fond of pears because they struck me as too mealy. Summer after summer that little pear tree turned out a crop of pears and I completely ignored them. Year after year the pears were there for the taking and I took none. Then one day when I was about eighteen I pushed the lawn mower past the tree and stopped. I looked at the tree as I had so many times before. But this time I figured, "Why not?" I took a pear and bit into it. "Not bad," I thought. "Why didn't I do this sooner?" I had another pear before going back to work and now I rather enjoy them.

That little tree is a lot like we are. We bear fruit. We have it available to meet people's needs. Sometimes there is a response, sometimes there is not. Sometimes, in the Lord's infinite wisdom, the timing takes eighteen years or longer. But, like that little tree, we are bearing fruit. We are living Spirit-filled Christian lives in the presence of other people. That is really what bearing fruit is all about . . . no more . . . no less.

Notes

[1] Henri Nouwen, *The Way of the Heart: Desert Spirituality and Contemporary Ministry* (New York: The Seabury Press, 1981), p. 31.

[2] John Daane, *Preaching with Confidence* (Grand Rapids, Mich.: Wm. B. Eerdmans Publishing Co., 1980), p.45.

[3]Elton Trueblood, *The New Man for Our Time* (New York: Harper & Row, Publishers Inc., 1970), p. 25.

[4]Ray Stedman, *Secrets of the Spirit* (Old Tappan, N.J.: Fleming H. Revell Co., 1975), pp. 85-86.

[5]David Wilkerson, with John and Elizabeth Sherrill, *The Cross and the Switchblade* (Old Tappan, N. J.: Fleming H. Revell Co., 1964), p. 118.

CHAPTER 6

Really Doing Something

"I am the vine, you are the branches. He who abides in me, and I in him, he it is that bears much fruit, for apart from me you can do nothing" (John 15:5).

Many years and, alas, even more pounds ago, I ran on the junior high track team. Early in my first season I developed a self-righteous, wishful theory. Drawing on Paul's teaching, "I can do all things in him who strengthens me" (Philippians 4:13) and Jesus' wisdom, "Apart from me you can do nothing," I reasoned I should win most, if not all, races. It only made sense. If I could do all things in Christ, then obviously I could win my heat of the fifty-yard dash. Add to that the fact that any runner who showed himself to be apart from Christ could do nothing, and I would seem to have had each sprint locked up.

My theory came with a ready-made testing system. Each race would be a proving ground. All I needed to do was separate the wheat from the chaff before the race began, and then see who won. My method centered on the conviction that any sprinter who used the Lord's name in vain obviously had an inner character flaw. He had revealed himself to be an utter heathen. Being a righteous man myself, I should conquer him when the starting gun sounded. It was to be predestination of the cinders. Since plenty of nervous banter filled the air around the starting blocks, and since the jittery jabber tended to be crude in tone, I had ample opportunity to test my hypothesis.

To my total delight the theory seemed to have substance. I won the first few races. Even when I finished second or third in a few later races, I managed to defeat the runners who I had decided ahead of time were godless. Those who managed to finish ahead of me, I merely elevated to the cherished and highly exclusive group: "Holier than I."

Then on a fateful Tuesday the big meet came along. The other school had a tall lanky fellow running in my heat. His size made me a bit nervous until I heard him talk. What a mouth this chap had! He used the Lord's name so often in a blasphemous way, I figured I had the race in the bag. Just fire the gun and let me demolish this scoundrel. It would be a holy war, with God on my side. That tall unrighteous critter would be like the chaff which the wind drives away (Psalm 1:4).

Unhappily I had not counted on the wind driving him away quite so fast and in the direction he wanted to go, at that. I can still see his back disappearing into a cinder cloud. I got clobbered. My self-righteousness got clobbered. My theory got clobbered. With Jeremiah I wondered, "Why does the way of the wicked prosper? Why do all who are treacherous thrive?" (Jeremiah 12:1). It made no sense to me that Jesus could have said, "Apart from me you can do nothing," when someone clearly apart from him had been able to do more than a godly man such as I.

This chapter would be a motivational gem in a worldly sense if I could write that owing to hard work and prayer, the day came when I raced that lanky dude again and trounced him soundly. But that would not be the truth. Reality records that I lost many more races in my less-than-stellar career and plenty of my losses were to nonbelievers. I was only beginning to learn in the school of hard knocks that there would be many times when the non-Christian beats the Christian.

The art of staying Christian takes into account the fact that ungodly persons may do extremely well in life. If we have naively premised our faith on the assumption that God will grant us special favors and cause everything to work out especially for us, we are doomed to disillusionment. We have set ourselves up for a fall. When we see how well people are doing who live in complete disregard of the teachings of Christ, our faith might crumble.

An old seminary chum, John Huffman, preached very eloquently on the psalmist's words: "Truly God is good to the upright, to those who are pure in heart. But as for me, my feet had almost stumbled, my steps had well nigh slipped. For I was envious of the arrogant, when I saw the prosperity of the wicked" (Psalm 73:1-3). He said,

> "Drop in on a southern Florida yacht club any Sunday morning of the year; you'll see well-tanned bodies, handsome, finely attired, setting out for a day of sailing in total disregard that it is the Lord's day. Hedonism is so attractive. Secularism has such an appeal. Every spare moment can go for recreation. You don't have to worry about God. You don't have to think about others. Entertain yourself. Have a good time. Wouldn't it be great? Here I am trying to be faithful to God and I've got my physical problems and that fellow seems to get all the breaks.
>
> "This wicked man seems so arrogant. He wears his pride as if it is a gold necklace flung casually around his neck. He owns the world. It's all his. And he'll walk over anyone who gets in his way."[1]

Make no mistake about it; the wicked do very well. Indeed, sometimes they do well because they do what is wrong, while we often suffer for the very reason that we do what is right. Their illegal or immoral actions occasionally permit them to beat us.

One morning in a suburb of Rochester, New York, I drove to the post office. Two relatively new structures stood near the street and in front of a village shopping plaza, adding character to an otherwise typical parking lot. A bank building stood just to the right of the post office. Between the buildings ran an access lane from the parking lot to the street and right beside it the driveway for the bank's drive-thru window. The village fathers and mothers spotted a traffic jam while the buildings were still on the drawing board. They wisely made both lanes one-way—out—and put two large "Do Not Enter" signs at the entrance, one on either side of the driveways.

On this particular morning traffic was heavy. As I approached the buildings, I saw that one parking space remained in the very small lot in front of the post office. Wanting to be a good citizen, I entered the plaza parking lot and drove the obstacle course behind the bank. Just as I had negotiated the last turn and was heading up the access lane, a woman in a station wagon came right through the "Do Not Enter" signs and took *my* space.

If thoughts do not count, I was a totally righteous man in that situation. Yes, I admit I thought of parking her in, but that would have been poor form, stooping to the illegal act of double parking. I confess that I thought of giving her a piece of my mind. But my mind needs all the pieces it can get, and besides, such behavior would be rather petty and trite. As I sat fuming, with fists clinched on the steering wheel, I realized I had been beaten out of a parking space because someone else broke the very law I was obeying. No doubt, if I had broken that law, I would have won out and gotten the space.

A wheelchair athlete by the name of Skip Wilkins helped me understand how a Christian such as I can get clobbered time and again by non-Christians and still claim the promises of Scripture.

Before a tragic accident sentenced him to life in a wheelchair, Skip had been an incredible high school athlete. With little exaggeration the term "superstar" was used to describe him. His records in track still stand and his prowess on the football field had earned him scholarships galore, the most appealing to him being one from Duke University in whose backfield he planned to excel. But a freak fall off water skis a few days after high school graduation left him a quadriplegic, lucky to be alive.

Skip somehow bounced back. Not only did he discover himself as a child of God, but he realized that God could use him even in a wheelchair.

A crippled athlete is still an athlete. While a lesser person would have moped and felt sorry for himself, Skip went into training. He pushed himself hard to get into the best shape he could, eventually rising to the point where he won a gold medal in the wheelchair olympics. He is justly proud of that moment and ably uses it as an introduction to young athletes.

Skip now has a ministry traveling around the country speaking in churches and schools, witnessing for Christ, and challenging all comers to table tennis, a sport in which his limited mobility does not prevent him from trouncing the best athletes in town.

It was at a pancake breakfast for senior highs that Skip really got through to me. He raised the question of how to reconcile the promises of Scripture with the realities of life. With a wisdom that had to be inspired, Skip gestured to a young man at the front table. "Hey," he said, "suppose I challenge you to a one-hundred-yard dash. You can be on foot and I'll be in the wheelchair." The image was absurd. Skip was hunched in his chair, the lad he was challenging looked eager and able to leap up and run ten laps around the gym without being winded. Skip was more than ready to play on the absurdity to make his point.

"Don't you think I would be abusing Paul's words 'I can do all things' if I said Paul promised me I would win that race?" Skip went on to explain that he has learned to accept his own limitations. He knows what he physically cannot do. He explained to us that when Paul made his statement, the apostle was not wanting us to assume we can all do absolutely everything, every time, in every place. Paul was talking about doing the Lord's work. Skip knew that he could not hope to win that race and had grown to the point in his life where he could live with that. But he knew that he could witness to Jesus Christ and help make Christ a living reality for agile teenagers who could run circles around him. His point struck home to this decrepit warrior of many races that had been lost behind the junior high gym.

My problem as a young Christian was that I applied biblical truth the wrong way. Jesus' statement "Apart from me you can do nothing" and Paul's teaching "I can do all things" have little if anything to do with fifty-yard dashes, or parking spaces, or a whole host of other episodes in life where we try to gain a secular edge on some adversary. Jesus was referring to *HIS* work. As I hope the reader is noting, I have tried in drafting this manuscript to put as much emphasis on the word "his" as I possibly can.

In our production-oriented society, emphasis on work is only natural. But it misses the truth. The trouble with work is that we measure it in terms of results, success or failure. We put it upon the scoreboard to gauge whether we are winning or losing. The trouble with work lies in the prickly point that non-Christians do "work" too and, as we have hinted, sometimes do it better than Christians. Non-Christians not only keep up with us in foot races, they also keep up with us in those endeavors we earmark "Done exclusively by Christians."

In his book *On Being Christian,* Hans Küng reflects on the dialogue with non-Christian religions and philosophies. He draws the following conclusion:

> Today others are not simply saying something different, but often the same thing. Non-Christians too are in favor of love, justice, a meaning to life, being good and doing good, humanity. And in practice they often go further than Christians in this respect. But if others say the same thing, what is the point of being a Christian? Today Christianity is involved everywhere in a *double confrontation*: with the great world religions on the one hand and with the non-Christian "secular" humanisms on the other. And today the question is thrust even on the Christian who has hitherto been institutionally sheltered and ideologically immunized in the Churches: compared with the world religions and modern humanisms, is Christianity something essentially different, really something special?[2]

What makes Christianity special is not the work—important as that may be. What makes Christianity essentially different and special is the HIS.

Familiar words from a Psalm helped me as I was groping for handles to get hold of this insight. Suddenly a light clicked on and I could see something I had been missing. "Unless the LORD builds the house, those who build it labor in vain" (Psalm 127:1). Do you see what the psalmist was saying? He was not proposing that no house could ever be built without God. Far from it. He was saying that apart from God a very well-crafted, elegant mansion might be built. But it would be in vain. The work, and the result of the work, is not the measure Scripture employs. The issue in our lives clearly is not so much what is done, as whose work it is.

Let's bring all this home to a practical application to our own churches. What does it really mean to be about HIS work? Do we emphasize the "his," or the work? As one wag put it, are we genuinely doing the work of the church, or are we merely busying ourselves with church work?

The late Dean Arthur Adams of Princeton penned these sentences that have constantly stood watch over my ministry:

> Success for a congregation, and for the pastor who serves it, is to be measured against the divine purposes for the church: worship and mutual nurture and witness. Quantitative norms can, obviously, not be developed for these goals. Since Christ mourned over the multitudes lost without a shepherd, since he went to the cross for all men, since he commanded his followers to make disciples of all peoples, it may be assumed that he is pleased to see large numbers of people respond to his love and take part in the life of his family on earth. But as there is joy in heaven over one sinner who repents, the solitary visit to a humble dwelling may be as important as preaching to thousands. It depends upon one's orders.
>
> The decaying structure in which a handful of young people gather from the streets to play, and occasionally to pray, may be the birthplace of God's new springtime for the earth. The soaring contemporary cathedral, with three services on Sunday morning, may do little more than support dubious secular values. It is equally possible, of course, that the cathedral beautifully serves divine ends, and the crumbling structure houses sterile delusions. The norm for success appears to be not, How much? but, How faithful to God's purposes?[3]

I take him to mean that a congregation can pack its sanctuary to overflow. The budget can be oversubscribed. A parking problem can develop, the choirs can need extra chairs in the loft, and the programs can keep the church lighted late every night. But if the Lord is not in it, ". . . those who build it labor in vain." The work, and the result of the work, is not what makes a church The Church. Yet we are constantly tempted in our congregations to make success the be-all and the end-all of our existence.

The point is Jesus.

There will be times when we doubt the promises of the Lord. There will be moments when all the evidence seems stacked against faith. We will see non-Christians getting ahead of us, doing better than we are. We will look at our lives, our families, our church and wonder why things aren't going better. We will wonder why, if we have faith, there appear to be such meager results. We will wonder if we are wasting our time. What is the point of it all? Why have we bothered all these years?

Remember this: If we are abiding in him and he in us, and our lives are his and our work is his, then regardless of how the present results appear to us, we can be absolutely sure of one thing. We are really doing something. Let's keep it his, and let's keep it up.

Notes

[1]John Huffman, "Why Pay the Price of Being a Christian When the Wicked Prosper?" sermon, April 24, 1977.

[2]Hans Küng, *On Being Christian* (Garden City, N.Y.: Doubleday and Company, Inc., 1976), p. 25.

[3]Arthur Merrihew Adams, *Pastoral Administration* (Philadelphia: The Westminster Press, 1964), p. 160.

CHAPTER 7

God's Answer to Prayer

"If you abide in me and my words abide in you, ask whatever you will and it shall be done for you. By this my Father is glorified, that you bear much fruit, and so prove to be my disciples" (John 15: 7-8).

A youth group leader was teaching his students about prayer and its results. He was emphatically stressing to a young athlete, "If you pray for victory before a baseball game, God will see to it that you win." Someone asked, "What if he loses?" The leader, without batting an eye, said that the loss would merely demonstrate that the player/prayer did not have enough faith. He then continued to hammer home his message that if you have faith, and if you pray correctly, you will definitely win. Someone asked the difficult question, "What happens if a Christian on the other team also prays faithfully and correctly for his team to win? Which team would win in those circumstances? Would the heavenly computer break down?" The group leader turned crimson. It had never occurred to him that there might be Christians on an opposing team, or that God might receive conflicting prayer requests.

Fortunately the group had a wit in its midst. He chimed in with a tension-relieving answer: "God, in his infinite wisdom, would see to it that it rained that day."

Our topic is prayer. How should a Christian pray and with what expectation?

Jesus tells us the answer in John 15:7 and 8. Read these two verses very carefully. "If you abide in me, and my words abide in you, ask whatever you will, and it shall be done for you. By this my father is glorified, that you bear much fruit, and so prove to be my disciples."

For most of us, certain words immediately jump off the page and stick to our brains, exciting our minds. "Ask whatever you will, and it shall be done for you." Were we to keep reading, a similar sort of experience would hit us at verse 16: " . . . so that whatever you ask the Father in my name, he may give it to you."

Is Jesus serious?

Evidently he is. Why else would he bring it up . . . twice? Enter these verses in our spiritual data banks alongside such promises as "Ask, and it will be given you; seek, and you will find; knock, and it will be opened to you" (Matthew 7:7), and this faith business sounds like a pretty good deal. Prayer will work every time. Make your prayer request, any request, and it will be granted.

I have been in the ministry long enough to know that we cannot move lightly past that thought. I have seen evidence which supports beyond any doubt the fact that Christians have called out to God in prayer and he has responded. I have seen persons ask and receive. I sometimes wonder how much more we could all receive from the Lord, if only we asked for it. As it is the nature of the vine to feed its branches, so it is the nature of the living Christ to feed us. "Ask and you will receive."

But watch out! We want so much to believe we will get what we want through prayer that we do not listen carefully to what Jesus actually said. We bury his message under an avalanche of our own wishes. Note this point carefully: Jesus did not guarantee that God would grant every request every time. Yes, God will always answer prayer. But the answer can be yes, no, or wait.

You may feel that I am quibbling, backing down from boldly

declaring the promises of God. You may be wondering how I could come on with this yes, no, wait line when I have just said that I knew from experience that God says yes when a Christian prays. What I actually said was that I have seen the prayer requests of Christians answered in the positive. I did not draw the conclusion that therefore *all* prayers get a yes. I am keenly aware from experience that just because one person prayed in a particular situation and received a certain answer does not mean another person with the same faith quotient will have the same prayer results in the same circumstances.

Though many persons seem to wish it were otherwise, in a worldly sense, God would not make a very good bureaucrat. Good bureaucrats always worry about precedents. "If we do this for him or her, we will have set a precedent and have to do it for everyone." "If we let you do that, then we will have to let everybody do it." God is no bureaucrat at all. He cannot be programmed, or predicted, or totally understood. He is God. He responds as he will, when he wills. To stay Christian we need to hold before us the truth that he wants us to ask, and he wants us to know that he is God. He never wants us to compare the answers we get with those our fellow Christians got. There is only harm in that. Just keep asking and know that he is God.

As the disciples leaned forward to catch his every word, Jesus set a context in which to understand what he meant by the phrase, "Ask whatever you will, and it shall be done for you." Without the context we cannot possibly hear what he really said. Lest these words get mangled by our self-centered wishes, let's protect them by wrapping around them the context Jesus chose.

1

First, Jesus worked to create a corporate setting. He had gathered a group and taught them to think in terms of a group analogy. The image of the vine and the branches tells each of us that we are only one among many. "I [singular] am the vine, you [plural] are the branches." By the time our Lord came to his teaching about prayer, the group dynamic had momentum. "You [as a group] ask whatever you [as a group] will. . . ."

One of my favorite verses in Scripture is 1 Corinthians 10:13, "He will not let you be tempted beyond your strength." I like it because it cannot be understood except in terms of the corporate Christian fellowship.

A woman came to me one day because her life was weighed down with problems. On top of everything else, Christians were making matters worse. "If I hear those 'super Christians' quote 1 Corinthians 10:13 one more time, I'll scream," she said. Evidently her church friends had been smugly quoting this verse to her, implying her troubles were not so bad. She could handle them. "God says you can cope." Their attitude was a double-edged sword that cut her deeply. On the one hand, they dropped the line on her and piously left her. "After all, if God will never give you more than you can handle, you can handle this. You don't need us." She was left isolated from support to sink or swim on her own. On the other hand, the cruel use of this verse made her feel guilty for being overwhelmed, as though her life were a repudiation of Scripture, or Scripture were a repudiation of her life.

What a burden was lifted when I reminded her that Paul was not writing to the one Christian in Corinth! He was writing to the many Christians. The letter was sent to a group. The "you" in the verse is plural. The Lord may or may not let individuals be confronted with more than they can handle alone. But God has promised that the Christian fellowship will have the strength to withstand temptations in its hour of testing. I advised her to admit her individual human frailty, admit that on her own she was overwhelmed. There was no need to feel guilty about that. I suggested she get more fully involved in prayerful fellowship. She did and was greatly helped as they carried her through her time of trial. Staying Christian means admitting how much we need other Christians to sustain us in our journey.

As we become immersed in the midst of fellowship, realizing that prayer, like Christianity, is not an individual sport, a fundamental dynamic of prayer will dawn on us. We will discover that no one of us is the only person on earth. We will become sensitive to the fact that our group or our fellowship does not make up the entire kingdom of God. In short, we will become mindful of the needs of others. This was the failing of the person who said, "Pray and you will win the game." He forgot there were other people around.

By beginning the Lord's Prayer with a plural, *Our* Father . . . ," Jesus was driving home to us how important it is to stay open to the voices of other people. When we realize the corporate nature of prayer, we are more receptive to his kingdom and his will. We realize that daily bread is for all of us. William Ramsay once wrote, "We cannot pray properly without putting others first. And we cannot put others first properly without praying for them."[1] How distressed our Lord must be at the failure of Christians to get beyond themselves and become sensitive to others!

James W. Silver wrote an analysis of the role of religion in the Civil War. One Christian's perception of a turn in the battle illustrated how provincial and self-centered our prayer life can be: "Late in the war Sherman's troops came within eight miles of Chester, South Carolina, 'but an All Wise Providence protected us' and turned them off on a different road to Lancaster. What the Lancastrians thought of this change in plans is not a matter of record."[2]

I encountered a similar attitude a few years ago. I was serving a church in York, Pennsylvania, when the scare at Three Mile Island occurred. From a hilltop near my house I could see the towers of the nuclear power plant where the "accident" had happened. Amid my memories of those trying days are the words of one man who commented to me about the fact that the wind was blowing away from York. "Oh John, the Lord is good," he said. "Whoever doesn't believe in prayer hasn't seen how the Lord is blowing all that radiation away from York." I was stunned! The man was rejoicing because he believed "the Lord" was blowing radiation over neighboring counties. The only thing that seemed to matter to this man's religious experience was that we didn't get any radiation blown on us.

I cannot and really ought not to have a fruitful prayer experience until I realize I am not the only person on the face of the earth.

2

Second, Jesus wanted the disciples to experience his invading presence in their prayers.

At this point, when I am speaking about John 15, I often play a dirty trick on the group. The reader will recall that a few pages ago I suggested that verses 7 and 8 be read very carefully. I then mentioned that the line "Ask whatever you will, and it shall be done for you" jumps out and grabs us. Now I would ask that the reader try to remember the words that came immediately before that phrase. Don't turn back. That's cheating. Most people cannot remember what the words are. Yet the words that came before are the condition that makes the promise possible. "If you abide in me and my words abide in you. . . . "

To bring home what this condition means, we need to ask ourselves a fundamental question: When we pray, whose prayer is it? The answer seems simple. One person after another will respond, "It is my prayer." We have the image of ourselves praying in one place to the Lord who is completely distinct from us, probably in another place.

But Jesus has a radically new understanding of prayer. He is saying, in effect, "Do not think prayer is your work, or your effort, or your words alone. When you pray, it is not just your prayer. It is also mine. If *my* words abide in you. . . . " To pray aright is to verbalize what happens when we have the mind of Christ within us. Prayer is Christ at work within me. It is his prayer through me.

In *The Silver Chair*, C. S. Lewis said of the world hereafter, "In that land you can't want the wrong things." I often hear people say they could quit smoking if they wanted to. They could give up booze if they wanted to. What they fail to realize is that they cannot want to. Jesus knows that what we want is determined deep within us, and he seeks to be present there as our Lord, influencing our desires and longings. To determine just how far I have let him into my life, I must ask myself, "Do I really want what Christ wants?" How my prayer is answered hangs on the answer to that question.

John Calvin wrote that "when He promises that he will grant whatever we wish, he does not give us leave to form wishes according to our own fancy. . . . He limits the wishes of his people to the rule of praying in a right manner, and that rule subjects, to the good pleasure of God, all our affections."[3] As one commentary put it, "Petitions prompted by the indwelling words of Jesus cannot fail to be in harmony with the Divine Will. A petitioner who 'abides in Christ' asks habitually 'in His Name,' *i.e.*, he asks as Christ would ask, and so his satisfaction is sure."[4]

It was my privilege, a few years ago, to work on an evangelistic venture with Dr. Myron Augsburger. One morning Myron spoke to a group of clergy. He shared the fact that many letters are pushed onto his desk for him to sign. Often these letters have been drafted by other people to be sent out over his signature. He told us that he had developed a policy never to affix his name to anything until he had read it carefully and agreed that the contents properly expressed his mind. If the letter did not, he would send it back to be redrafted.

His point applies very clearly to prayer. We Christians often send a message to God, signing it with Jesus' signature. We sign off, "In the name of Jesus Christ, Amen." Myron asked if we had ever thought seriously about what it means to dictate a prayer as if it were a letter and send it to God over Jesus' signature without making sure the prayer properly expresses the mind of Christ. Sadly, most of us had not. But from that day to this, I have, and what a difference it makes!

3

Third, Jesus set a context which would allow the disciples to know exactly what to pray for. William Ramsay wrote, "In short, Jesus seems very little interested in how we pray. But He is enormously interested in what we pray for."[5]

The whole analogy of the vine and its branches showed the disciples that the purpose of the vine was to bear fruit through the branches. Indeed the branches' reason for being was to let the fruit happen. Prayer, then, is to be understood as an act of branches calling forth the purpose of the vine through them.

Biblical scholars stress that we should combine verses 7 and 8. Though they seem on the surface to be tracking two different concepts, the verses have a common theme at heart. When Jesus is abiding in our prayers, our prayers become petitions that we might bear fruit. "If you abide in me and my words abide in you, ask whatever you will, and it shall be done for you. By this my Father is glorified, that you bear much fruit, and so prove to be my disciples."

Hollis Haff serves as chaplain for the Pittsburgh Steelers football team. In addresses to church groups in the Pittsburgh area, Hollis is fond of saying, "God has never promised His assistance to the Steelers to win another Super Bowl. But He has promised His assistance in helping them make people disciples and He has promised His assistance to everyone else for the same mission." In Pittsburgh many people root for and no doubt pray for the Steelers. There's nothing wrong with that. The Lord wants to hear all our prayers, as long as we remember that Jesus is not promising in John 15 that God will jump to attention and get wins for our favorite football team whenever we fervently pray for them.

God's promise is that he will aid his people when they pray that their lives might bear fruit. When you and I want to provide spiritual nourishment for others or meet human needs, or live lives filled with love, joy, and peace, God has promised that, if we pray for these, he will hear our prayers and according to his timetable, it will be done. We can pray without any doubt. We can be absolutely sure on this one. Even if the initial evidence appears for a time completely counter to what we had hoped, we can trust the Lord. He has promised to grant every prayer which in faith asks that we might bear fruit.

Prayer is something Jesus asks us to do. He asks us to ask. Prayer is turning the key in the ignition. It starts the spiritual motor. It opens the doors so that the life of Jesus Christ might more fully surge through us. As James Jauncey put it, "It is quite evident that unless we pray for some things, they will never be accomplished."[6] Praying to bear fruit is an essential. Raymond Brown suggests that the verb "to ask" in verse 7 is most likely in the imperative. Jesus expects us to do it, indeed requires it. Pray that the divine purpose of bearing fruit might happen in your lives, and it will, and God will be glorified and you will prove to be his disciples.

Helen Shoemaker tells of a woman whose prayers about circumstance seemed not to have been heeded. But her blessing came in that her prayers to bear fruit were heeded indeed.

I was having tea with Marie before a cozy, crackling fire in her big, comfortable, old-fashioned living room. She was knitting, and we were talking enthusiastically about all kinds of people and projects in which we were mutually interested. But nothing in Marie's look or manner betrayed the fact that she knew she was dying of cancer. She was in constant pain and the doctor had given her a year to live.

Her friends and relatives prayed for her continually—for healing, for peace, for freedom from fear, for a continued sense of her Lord's presence. The first prayer he did not grant: she was not healed. The others were granted in abundant measure. In a letter Marie wrote to me before her death, she told how completely she had been freed from fear. I will never forget her closing sentence: "I have one great assurance, that underneath are the everlasting arms and that no matter what happens, they will always be there." In answer to prayer, God gave Marie peace of mind, and she faced pain and death with courage and confidence.[7]

Notes

[1]William Ramsay, "Priorities and People," *Presbyterian Outlook*, January 31, 1977, p. 13.

[2]James W. Silver, *Confederate Morale and Church Propaganda* (New York: W. W. Norton & Company, Inc., 1967), p. 15.

[3]John Calvin, *Commentary on the Gospel According to John*, v. 2 (Grand Rapids, Mich.: Baker Book House, 1981), p. 11.

[4]J. H. Bernard, *A Critical and Exegetical Commentary on the Gospel According to St. John*, v. II (Edinburgh: T. and T. Clark, 1963), p. 482.

[5]Ramsay, *op cit.*, p. 13.

[6]James H. Jauncey, *The Compelling Indwelling* (Chicago: Moody Press, 1972), p. 56.

[7]Helen S. Shoemaker, *Prayer and Evangelism* (Waco, Tex.: Word Books, 1974), p. 76; used by permission of Word Books, Waco, Texas 76796.

CHAPTER 8

God Is for Us

"As the Father has loved me, so have I loved you; abide in my love" (John 15:9).

Jesus was quite concerned about what the disciples might think of his Father. Skilled at reading the thoughts of those around him, he may have sensed they harbored a false impression. Perhaps their minds had fixed on the image of the Father as an exacting gardener coming at them, pruning knife in hand, an image that made them want to shrink from his presence. Jesus wanted to make sure they had an accurate picture.

Yes, he is an exacting judge and his judgment is to be taken seriously, but there is much more to the Father than that. We Christians need to stay on the alert lest we separate the Father from the Son, making an angry judge of the Father and portraying the Son as an independent agent who came to us, driven by his own sense of compassion, to help us argue our case against the Father. It is easy to imagine Jesus being the good guy who defends us and to imagine the Father being the bad guy who wants to send us to hell. Jesus never intends Christians to think so ill of his Father.

John spotted this concern. He was impressed by the number of times the Lord told his disciples that he and his heavenly Father were on the same team. "He who has seen me has seen the Father" (John 14:9). "I and the Father are one" (John 10:30). Without wanting to lecture those in the Upper Room on systematic theology, Jesus at least wanted them to know they could not play him against his Father. They could begin to grasp Christianity only when they gained a full appreciation of the Father and what he was doing through the Son.

Verse 9 is a turning point: the analogy of the vine and branches phases out and teachings on love come into focus. "As the Father has loved me, so have I loved you; abide in my love." At the top of the turn Jesus wants us to appropriate a biblical truth about love. The Source is beyond us and beyond our earthly relationships. Wherever love surrounds us, we know that a gift has been given by the Father. He is the Original Lover, the Creator who makes it happen, the Producer behind every genuine love scene in history. Despite the modern idiom, you can't make love. Only God can.

Jesus taught his disciples that love is a chain reaction, touched off by the Father. "As the Father has loved me, so have I loved you." Some people have thought Jesus was saying he loved in the same way the Father did. This interpretation, however, avoids the thrust of what Jesus believed. It misses the extent to which he saw his Father as the trigger in the whole process. Love is of God. While love is not God, God is love. Stay close to the Source. Jude put it quite succinctly: "Keep yourselves in the love of God" (Jude 21).

About to graduate his disciples and send them into a world that could be cold and cruel, Jesus wanted them to know the Father. There would always be a temptation to let circumstance define God. Pain can make us dislike the Father, make us believe he has a sinister sadism about him. The tragedies of life can leave one with an unflattering impression of the Creator. In the down times people say things which they don't mean but which nonetheless stay with them, festering at the depth of their souls. In short: A believer might be drawn to the conclusion that "since my life is terrible and God is the

Lord of my life, God must be terrible for letting all this happen. I don't like a God who is terrible. Therefore I no longer accept him. I do not want to be counted among his people anymore. Just count me out." As one woman put it to her minister after a personal tragedy, "Pastor, I think you should be the first to know. I have just fired God!"

Little wonder Jesus wanted to imprint permanently on the cranium of every one of his people an indelible image of the Father. "No matter what happens, this is what God is like. Don't dare forget it!" Again and again he drives it home. God loves us. The love we see anywhere in the universe has had its genesis in the Father. He cares. He would give anything on our behalf, including his only Son. No matter where we are and no matter what we face, God loves us, shares our joys and our sorrows. Martin Luther thought of God as a glowing oven full of love. *We will not stay Christian by clinging only to a pleasant image of Jesus. Our endurance in the faith will depend on whether we have a vital walk with the Father.*

We began our exploration of "How to Stay Christian" with the two-word phrase "I am." We traced it back to the burning bush by which Moses asked God to introduce himself, and God said, "Yahweh." God meant for that name to be open-ended. He never meant the cryptic "I am who I am" to be Moses' final understanding of theology. As a word, "Yahweh" points forward to what is coming. It can mean "I will be what I will be." In effect, God was saying to Moses, "You will really get to know me on the basis of what you will see me do." As Dr. William Albright wrote, "He Causes to be what Comes into Existence."[1]

So it was that when Yahweh reintroduced himself in the preface to the Ten Commandments, he had earned the right to more than "I am that I am." He could legitimately say, "I am the Lord your God, who brought you out of the land of Egypt, out of the house of bondage" (Exodus 20:2).

I like that. I find that I am strengtened in moments that might otherwise undermine my faith because I know the Lord of my life is a God of action. Staying Christian is easier because my heart has been moved and my life changed by what he has done. He has proved himself. He has shown himself in actions that speak louder than words. I know for a fact that he loves me because I know what he has already done for me. I am not talking about the relative material success I have always enjoyed. It really does not cost God anything for me to be physically comfortable. I mean more than that, so much more. I am talking about what he has done for me that has cost him dearly.

I believe that all of what Jesus wanted to drum into his disciples is summed up best in the four words of Romans 8:31: "God is for us." If we want a phrase to carry with us into life, a phrase for waking up in the morning, for heading off to our daily pursuits, for facing the challenges that come our way, hang on to those four words, "God is for us."

Journey to the heart of the gospel and meet the God who is radically for us. He has given. "God so loved the world that he gave . . . " (John 3:16). Paul writes that God loved us so much that he did not spare his own Son but gave him up for us all. The prophet Isaiah foretold "for unto us a child is born, unto us a son is given" (Isaiah 9:6, KJV). Note the words "unto us." God did not put his Son on display in a window behind bulletproof glass. He did not put Jesus on a pedestal for all the world to see. Jesus was not on loan. He did not have "Handle with Care" stamped on his forehead. God gave him over to us to do with as we pleased, no strings attached. "God so loved the world that he gave his only begotten Son."

To appreciate how totally God gave his Son, think of that hot, dusty afternoon, a Friday, when Jesus hung on a cross. My wife and I find Salvador Dali's painting of the crucifixion powerful because it looks down from above, perhaps as God might have seen it. As parents who want to dash out into the yard every time one of our children appears victimized by unfair play, we find it almost impossible to understand the anguish that must have mingled with compassion in the heart of God as he, the Lord of the universe, held back his power while a misguided, unjust mob nailed Jesus to a cross and lifted it up on the brow of Golgotha. "He did not spare his own Son. . . . "

But then let your mind drift ahead a few days to Easter Sunday. Yes, it was a victory celebration, yet there was no sense of getting even. The words, "Didn't we show them who's boss around here?" could not be heard. The full impact of

God's love for us at Easter time came home in a passage delivered by John Claypool at Yale's Lyman Beecher Lectures:

> They took your son in and received him cordially at first. But then very quickly their mood changed, and they became sullen and hostile. Just yesterday they took him out behind the barn, tied his hands and tortured him for a while, and then killed him in cold blood.
>
> As I allowed myself to feel the emotions of such a situation, I found a primitive rage building up in me against the creatures who would do this sort of thing. My first impulse was to unleash all the hurtful and destructive powers within me against such utter ingrates. I had to admit that if it had been in my power to raise my son back from the dead, it would never in a thousand years have occurred to me to send him back to the kind of creatures who had treated him this way.
>
> At that point, the miracle of the Easter event broke over me. It was not just the power of God that astonished me here—the ability to take something that had been killed and call it back to life again. That is amazing. But even more amazing is the patience and mercy of a God who would still have hope for the kind of creatures who had treated his only begotten Son that way. Three days after human beings killed him in cold blood, the word was out, not only that he was alive again, but that he was saying, "I go before you into Galilee. Let's keep on keeping on. Let's get back to the task of dispelling suspicion and reconciling the world back to the Father as he really is." That is the towering miracle of Easter that broke in on me that day.
>
> The story the Christian preacher has to tell is the story of a God whose only reason for creating was his desire to share the wonder of his aliveness and who . . . has refused to stop loving or to give up on creation, but moves to repair the damage and to affirm again that he really is for us and not against us.[2]

It was a God who had shown his love through the agonizing self-giving of the cross and resurrection that Paul had in the front of his mind as he wrote the famous words in Romans 8. Paul had been around. His faith had been tested in the crucible with evil elements and violent reactions. He remained a follower of Jesus Christ through it all because he had been gripped by the tenacious power of the Father's love. "What then shall we say to this? If God is for us, who is against us? He who did not spare his own Son but gave him up for us all, will he not also give us all things with him?" (Romans 8:31-32).

Martin Niemöller was one of many Christians who witnessed

to Jesus Christ in prison. During World War II, he was held at the Nazi prison camp at Dachau. He was spared execution only by the timely arrival of the Allied Forces. On Christmas Eve 1944, he said this in his sermon: "In Christ, God himself brings the deliverance which we were unable to secure for ourselves. He not only inclines towards us, but lifts us toward himself: 'I will forgive their iniquity, and I will remember their sin no more!' (Jeremiah 31:34). Christ, the 'God with us,' is also the 'God for us,' and we may joyfully cry out, 'if God is for us, who is against us?' " (Romans 8:31).[3]

Circumstance never defines God. God defines God. He is who he is, or better than that, he is who he has proved himself to be in Christ. We have come to know the secret of his inner nature. Yes, that's right. He is for us. And "if God is for us, who is against us?"

Notes

[1]William F. Albright, *From the Stone Age to Christianity* (Baltimore: Johns Hopkins Press, 1940), p. 198.

[2]John R. Claypool, *The Preaching Event* (Waco, Tex.: Word Books, 1980), pp. 49-50; used by permission of Word Books, Waco, Texas 76796.

[3]Martin Niemöller, *Dachau Sermons,* trans. Robert H. Pfeiffer (New York: Harper & Row, Publishers, Inc., 1946), p. 12.

CHAPTER 9

To Be an Enduring Fellowship of Love

"This is my commandment, that you love one another as I have loved you. Greater love has no man than this, that a man lay down his life for his friends. You are my friends if you do what I command you. No longer do I call you servants, for the servant does not know what his master is doing; but I have called you friends, for all that I have heard from my Father I have made known to you. You did not choose me, but I chose you and appointed you that you should go and bear fruit and that your fruit should abide; so that whatever you ask the Father in my name, he may give it to you. This I command you, to love one another" (John 15:12-17).

Jesus' teachings on love came back to John throughout his life. It was John who had a revelation on the Isle of Patmos and recorded what the risen Christ said to the church at Ephesus. "You have abandoned the love you had at first" (Revelation 2:4). The message to the Ephesians was not that they needed to be more chummy or practice gimmicks to develop a friendlier congregation. Their problem was that the love of

God no longer radiated from the center of their fellowship. The Source was missing. The warning to the Ephesians was ominous. In the language of the last book of the Bible they were told that their lamp stand would be removed. This was a symbolic way of saying, "If your first love does not return, you will cease to be the church. You can go through your motions, have your liturgies and your ecclesiastical procedures, but that which makes you the church will have vanished from your midst." The love of God at work among us is that important.

Christian tradition has it that John lived out his last days in Ephesus. In his declining years he was so weak that he had to be carried to church. We can imagine the tremendous aura of respect that must have surrounded him in that congregation. Here was a person who had actually been with Jesus. Little wonder that at the close of their worship services they invited John to say a few words. Every time he said the same thing: "Little children, love one another." Someone once asked him why he said only that and said it repeatedly. He answered, "Because this is our Lord's commandment and if we all fulfill this, nothing more is needed."

Our task as Christians is to draw on the Source and let love happen in our churches. If we want to stay Christian, we had better act on the truth that "love . . . endures all things" (1 Corinthians 13:7). "Little children, love one another."

As a way of giving shape to our discussion, I have elected to list six principles, all of which provide help for one who wants to stay Christian, for one who wants to abide in an enduring fellowship of love.

1. *Love Defined.* We came out of our last chapter with a working definition that I believe cuts to the core of *agape* love: God is for us. John wrote, "Beloved, if God so loved us, we also ought to love one another" (1 John 4:11). God's love flows through our words and deeds when we are for each other.

I had not realized the power of this thought in practical terms until I took my two older children bowling. In the first two games both kids rolled scores that were on the borderline between average and mediocre. Throughout all the frames the air was punctuated with a steady stream of sibling jabbing.

"You stink!" "You jerk, you blew it!" "You hold the ball wrong, you dummy!" "I think your name ought to be Gutterball!" I began to observe the boomerang effect of negative criticism. One youngster had called the other a "jerk" for rolling the ball poorly. Not only did that deflate the vulnerable one whose *faux pas* was now public record, but it also put pressure on the critical name-caller who was about to roll and feared making the same mistake and earning the same handle: "jerk!" Both kids were tightening up, their games disintegrating.

Something had to be done and it fell to me to play the role of helpful parent, figuring out what to do. By some miracle I got the two of them to believe they were on the same team. I don't recall if I offered a prize for their combined score or if I pitted their combined score against mine. Whatever I did, it worked. The name-calling stopped instantly. For a while at least they were totally for each other. Encouragement began. "You can do it." "Good job." "Don't worry, you'll do better next time." "Concentrate on this roll." I would not have believed it if I had not seen it with my own two eyes. Their scores went up thirty points each!

When we are among people who encourage us, who are for us, our lives change. We blossom. God intends that it be that way.

2. *Love as Command*. Jesus said, "This is my commandment, that you love one another . . . this I command you, to love one another" (John 15:12 and 17). American culture may have a rough go of accepting the fact that love is a command. We have been schooled to believe just the opposite. We glamorize the dating/mating process, believing that love is a romantic experience or at least something one chooses voluntarily. We "fall in love." We decide to say, "I love you." The net result is mass confusion over what love means. As one wag had it, "Love is the feeling you feel when you feel you're about to feel a feeling you have never felt before." I wish that definition were as foreign to modern experience as it is bizarre. Alas, too many people believe that love is something you feel when you feel like it. How many relationships split up on the matter-of-fact statement "I just don't feel it any more"?

Madeline L'Engle has brought to the surface the real problem with this popular thinking. "If love is a feeling, it is self-centered. It is awareness of ourselves and our own reactions. Love is not an emotion, it's policy."

There we have it. Love is policy. It is the law. Jesus commanded it. The Bible never teaches that we should love just when we feel like it. This is a matter of law. Jesus made love a law so that it could be stripped away from the control of our feelings and not be self-centered. Jesus made it law so that it could become "other centered" policy, regardless of how we feel about a particular person at a particular time.

Have you ever considered the magnitude of the apology Christendom owes its Christ that he had to make a command of love? He gave so totally of himself for us and we do not *naturally* give of ourselves in response. He had to command us to do it. What an embarrassment!

What a tragedy that our churches not only have to be commanded to do what should have come naturally, but that they also too often ignore the command that should not have been needed in the first place. In chapter 12 we will take up the matter of how hard it is to stay Christian when the world hates you. Let me tell you now, folks, it is harder to stay Christian when church people fail to love you than it is when the world hates you. The greatest danger to your faith may be a person in your own church. You can handle a declared atheist because you know what to expect. But a fellow Christian, who you thought would love you and accept you, can undo you. The slights, the put-downs, the opposition we get in church can be devastating to our faith. I have no idea, and don't think I want to know, of the number of persons whose faith I have jeopardized by an offhanded remark or an uncaring act. We all need to confess our sins on this one and struggle to do better in the future.

If you, the reader, really want to take seriously the business of staying Christian, I strongly suggest you start discussion in your church of how your fellowship can be more obedient to Christ's command to love. He gave the command because he knows we need it. He knows the church can be a source of strength or destruction, depending on how obedient we are to his commandment.

3. *Love Directed.* Jesus wants us to obey the command to love within our own churches. That's right: love church people.

Loving one another means that the next time we are in the sanctuary of our church or in a Bible study or attending a committee meeting, we need to look around, look at our fellow church members. These are the ones we are commanded to love. We're supposed to be for them. If love weren't a command but a suggestion, we could pick and choose persons to be recipients of our love. We might single out twenty or thirty people in the community to be for, and no doubt some of them would be in the church, though many would not. But love is a defined commandment that starts in the church. We are commanded first to love, of all creatures on this good earth, church people.

Many of us, I suspect, are like the junior highs in the child-care department. Junior highs offer their services as volunteer helpers. Why not? It gets them out of going to Sunday church school or church services. These twelve- and thirteen-year-olds decide to do the adults a favor and help with the little tots. But their help is negligible. The adults soon learn that most junior highs gravitate to babies that are (a) cute and cuddly; (b) not crying or sniffling; and (c) most important of all, clad in clean diapers. The not-so-cute, crying infants with messy diapers are avoided like the plague. It is as though they did not exist.

We have a tendency to gravitate to the lovable ones. A church has two shut-ins. One is visited by six people every week, the other is virtually ignored. "We don't call on her because she makes us feel so unpleasant." Oh, those feelings again! Remember that love is a command to be obeyed, whether we like it or not. Obedience means loving the cantankerous ones, the ornery ones, the bitter ones, the cliquish ones, the ones whose theology is different from ours, the gossipy ones. We have no choice in the matter. Jesus commands it.

4. *Love as Support.* Jesus was about to send out his disciples. He knew that as individuals they would not be able to survive in a hostile world unless the loving was good on the church home front. They needed to stay together. They needed the support of a fellowship to carry them through. For this reason the command to love not only binds us together, but also makes each one of us responsible to care for the other.

We are responsible for creating an environment to which

members of the fellowship can turn for support and encouragement. Unhappily, Christ's command calls us to alter many of our ways. Instead of sitting in church spotting who is being hypocritical, or who has some nerve to show up for worship, or who we wish would drop out so that we can have a better church, it is for us to let all members of the church know that we are pulling for them, cheering for them. Can persons come to our churches and honestly feel that we want them to grow stronger in their faith? If not, why are we disobeying the command of Christ?

Christ's command means we have to raise our threshold of write-off. Suppose that a man has not been to church for months and someone makes a motion at a committee meeting that we write him off. Have we forgotten that Christ's command makes that man the object of our love, not one to be written off? We are ordered to extend every possible effort to bring that man back to a place in the church family. Sadly, the very persons who need us the most we often write off the quickest. When a person has suffered a public humiliation and cannot come to church expecting support, we have broken the command of Christ. When a woman has been the victim of violence and no one in church will listen to her and try to understand her in her moment of anguish, we have sinned by breaking the command of Christ. We Christians need to pull together and support one another no matter what.

5. *Love Possessed.* We are comfortable saying of a gifted musician, "He's really got it." We observe a young person in one of the professions and conclude, "She's got what it takes." Athletes have it; politicians have it. The special ones possess a certain quality that separates them from the rest.

We are not quite so comfortable thinking of love as a possession, something a person "has." But that is precisely the way Jesus put it. "Greater love *has* no man than this. . . . " Paul speaks of love as a gift of the Spirit, given for building up the church. We are told to seek the higher gifts, and love is the highest of them all. Love is something given to us by the Lord to be used in his honor.

A minister friend confided in me the reason why he had to fire a member of the church staff. Frankly I had wondered about the action when it occurred because I had met the person and had been impressed. This was an individual with a wealth of talent, a brilliant young man with vast skills. "I had to fire him," my friend lamented. "He simply did not have any love for people. No matter how good he appeared, if he didn't have love, he couldn't minister."

Love is something you have, isn't it?

6. *Love as Example*. "Greater love has no man than this, that he lay down his life for his friends." Jesus did that. He gave his life for us and showed what love in its fullest is all about. It is not enough simply to say we are for another person. The question is, "What are we prepared to do about it?"

I stood in the hallway of a hospital, whispering with an emotionally drained and physically exhausted parent. A small child lay desperately ill on a bed barely visible through a partially open door. "I would give anything if I could be the one on that bed instead of my baby." These were not idle words offered to make a deal with God or impress the minister. This was total and honest commitment. This was a person who loved so much he wanted to jump out of his own skin and take on the form of that little baby. He was a parent who would sacrifice a healthy body for one that might be dying.

Love is like that. Love is so much for the other that we would actually bear the other's burdens (Galatians 6:2). Jesus did that for you and for me on the cross. He has shown that he is for us, and he wants us to show that kind of love in our churches. Jesus knew that a fellowship bound together in that way could stand the test of time.

CHAPTER 10

When We Obey

"If you keep my commandments, you will abide in my love. . . . These things I have spoken to you, that my joy may be in you. . . . You are my friends if you do what I command you. No longer do I call you servants, for the servant does not know what his master is doing; but I have called you friends, for all that I have heard from my Father I have made known to you" (John 15:10a, 11, 14, 15).

I fancied myself quite a mathematician until I entered my freshman year in college and enrolled in Calculus 103. The first test covered reasonably familiar ground and I passed. But from then on it was failure city. The instructor would meet with me after class to try drumming the material into my head with patient personal attention. Upperclassmen took me aside to lay out the secret of the course. I heard certain seemingly magic words uttered so often I could spout them from memory. But I still did not really understand what calculus was all about. Night after night I stared at the math book to no avail. I went over the problems and saw how the correct answer had been derived. Still it made no sense. Then, one afternoon about ten days before the final exam, a light went on in my brain. I understood. I could think in calculus. My mind was suddenly on the inside of the subject. I did well enough in the final to eke out a passing grade for the course.

Christianity is a lot like calculus for many people. They hear the words, learn some of the correct things to say, but their lives are not on the inside. The light has not gone on. To pursue the analogy further, Jesus' command to be for others is our homework. The Teacher is confident that as we do our lessons, a light will click on in our heads. We will be able to think in Christian terms. As John Newton put it, I " . . . was blind, but now I see."

In the section on love, verses 9-17, Jesus carefully intersperses a list of benefits that accrue to obedience. When we follow his command to love, we experience life in a way we would otherwise have missed. He outlines how our eyes are opened and we experience new realities with him.

Verse 10, "If you keep my commandments, you will abide in my love. . . ." Jesus now brings together his twin imperatives: abiding and loving. Earlier, remember, we discovered that abiding is best defined as openness to the will of God, letting God's will happen through our lives. Add to that our more recent discovery that God's will is to be for us, and we see how loving (being for others) is God's will at work in us. To love is to abide; to abide is to love.

Have you ever noticed that spiritual gifts are rarely given to us for our own use? The Lord gives individuals gifts so that they can serve others. Gifts are for the upbuilding of the fellowship. When we think of a person who has the gift of healing, we almost never think of that person laying hands on his or her own ailment. Our image is of the faith healer laying hands on someone else. God works in one person's life for the benefit of another person. If you and I should decide to live completely for ourselves, why should the Spirit give us anything or be actively at work in us?

John learned his lessons well. When he wrote his first letter, he included this: "If we love one another, God abides in us and his love is perfected in us. By this we know that we abide in him and he in us, because he has given us of his own Spirit.

. . . If any one says, 'I love God,' and hates his brother, he is a liar; for he who does not love his brother whom he has seen, cannot love God whom he has not seen" (1 John 4:12-13, 20). Or, "If you keep my commandments [to love], you will abide in my love."

I once heard an evangelist describe an episode he had with a college girl working as a summer intern in one of his ministries. On a hot August morning after chapel she asked to see him for a few moments. During the conversation she confided that her faith had gone flat. No crisis had occurred, but the air had definitely gone out of her sails. The enthusiasm with which she had begun the summer had been spent, and she was wondering if she could honestly stay on for the last few weeks if her heart wasn't in her work.

In what may seem like a rather callous move, he brushed her off, told her he sympathized with her but really did not have time to go into all of her problems just then. He was swamped and needed help. Come to think of it, could she pitch in? An elderly woman living in a tenement apartment was expecting a few items to be delivered and she was so lonely it would be wonderful if the person delivering the items could stay with her for a few hours just to offer companionship and a listening ear. Still in a blue mood, the coed reluctantly agreed to go and moped out of the office.

Wouldn't you know it! A few days later the girl bounded back into that same office, her face filled with an ear-to-ear grin. The answer to his question of how things were going was written in her expression. Depression and doubt and that old drab feeling were things of the past. A fresh breeze was sweeping across her life. This was an eager person ready to minister. Her only regret now was that the summer would end so soon. She told the evangelist that she really did not need to talk to him anymore. She couldn't figure out what had happened, but she thanked him for his time anyway.

As you might have guessed, that cagey fellow had not been all that busy when the girl first came into his office. The elderly woman in the tenement could certainly have used a visit but not nearly as much as the coed needed it. The evangelist had discerned that the girl was at a point in her discipleship where she needed to love, to be for someone. As she left his office the second time, he quietly thanked Jesus for keeping His promises, "If you keep my commandments, you will abide in my love. . . ."

Verse 11, "These things I have spoken to you, that my joy may be in you, and that your joy may be full." The phrase "These things I have spoken to you" crops up so often we can read it as a code. Seeing it, we know that Jesus is summing up, uttering the bottom line, saying, "Here's the point." All the words about abiding, bearing fruit, loving—all of them—were for the purpose of his joy glowing within us and our joy being full. As the Westminster Divines had it, "Man's chief end is to glorify God, and to enjoy him forever."

Reader, beware! Do not think about this one for very long. Our joy has a way of self-destructing in the heat of our own gaze. John Stuart Mill one time reflected that whenever he asked himself if he was happy, he ceased to be as happy as he had been before he asked the question. He's got something there. To wonder if I am happy is to focus on myself. For that instant I become the center of the stage. As Scripture teaches and experience bears out, I cannot be the center of my own attention and genuinely happy at the same time. Real happiness, akin to joy, is thus hard to pin down and is prone to disappear under personal scrutiny.

Joy is a fruit. This means it is a by-product, not something we seek as an end in itself. It is the Lord's gift to us, as we lose ourselves in his service. Joy comes when we aren't looking for it. It creeps up on us when we have forgotten ourselves and are living for others. It is only sometime later, as we think back on our experience, that we can honestly say, "I was quite happy then. It was good. That is what joy is all about."

Earl Palmer picked up this notion in his commentary on John's Gospel. "The Greek word *chara,* 'joy,' is related to the word *charis,* 'grace.' It has about it a sense of surprise and excitement. Jesus is teaching us that the result of our obedience to his will for life results in the exciting and liberating experience of his love—'that your joy may be full' (v.11). Joy is the virtue continuously promised to us by the world, but in reality it is 'the gigantic secret of the Christian.'"[1]

What then can I write about joy? How shall I describe it? Perhaps I should not try. It is not a word that should be described for a person who has not experienced it. That would be like describing a sunset to a man born blind. No. Joy is not a word in search of a definition. Rather we have an experience with Christ that is in search of a word. What shall we say it is like to have Christ alive within us? "Love?" . . . Yes, that is correct. "Peace?" . . . Yes, that is right also. "Joy?" . . . Yes, that's it! That is precisely it! Joy!

Verse 14, "You are my friends if you do what I command you." Friendship. For some destructive reason we have come to believe that friendship is an alternative to love. I can still remember a note I received from an attractive blonde in junior high school. I had a crush on her, but my puppy love was unrequited. She wished I had never been born. As a way of ending the relationship, which had never really begun, she wrote me a note: "Let's just be friends."

I have seen several examples on television or across a movie screen, where a relationship between a man and a woman begins to develop and he says to her, "Okay, Baby, this is where the friendship ends and the romance begins." Whereupon they kiss. The message conveyed is popular but dangerous. If the friendship ends when the romance begins, the romance will not last long. Any relationship that is not built and maintained on friendship is terminal. I tell couples contemplating marriage that friendship is the foundation of their life together. Of all the New Testament words for love, *phileo* (friendship) is the least appreciated and most lacking in our lives today. "You are my friends if you do what I command you."

A Texas minister has written, "When I left my old friend yesterday, I couldn't help reflecting on the observation of Daniel J. Levenson [sic], whose book, *The Seasons of a Man's Life*, is a more scholarly version of the best-selling book *Passages*. After interviewing forty men who went through crises during mid-life transition, he says, 'In our interviews, love, marriage, work, occupation were considered, but friendship was largely noticeable by its absence.' How few men, American at any rate, seem to have close and deep friendships."[2] I fear the same could be said of women.

I am convinced that a major reason why we are a society with so few friendships originates in our failure to put friendship and love together. We need to be reminded that *phileo* is not an alternative to loving. It is loving. When we think of friendship as inferior to love, we fail to realize that there is a cost to being friends. While acquaintances pass by us in a rather superficial way and are dismissed with a pleasant "Have a nice day," friendships occupy a central place in our lives and help direct our behavior. I put myself out for my friends because I am for them. Someone once said that a real friend is someone you can call at two in the morning without getting cussed out. Friends are for each other and stand ready to drop everything and rush to help when they are needed. In a very real sense, my friends have more control of my schedule than I do.

Jesus wants us to know that when we are obedient to him, we become his friends. His promise is that as we follow his lead, he will open our eyes to who he is, and do it in a way that will draw us more fully into an intimate walk with him. When we follow our own lead, we live for ourselves, by ourselves. But when we have the humble obedience of a man like Albert Schweitzer, we experience a closeness with our God that is impossible for persons who chase after anything less.

Schweitzer closed his epic book *The Quest of the Historical Jesus* with these words: "He comes to us as One unknown, without a name, as of old, by the lake-side, He came to those men who knew Him not. He speaks to us the same word: 'Follow thou me!' and sets us to the tasks which He has to fulfil for our time. He commands. And to those who obey Him, whether they be wise or simple, He will reveal Himself in the toils, the conflicts, the sufferings which they shall pass through in His fellowship, and, as an ineffable mystery, they shall learn in their own experience Who He is."[3]

Verse 15, "No longer do I call you servants, for the servant does not know what his master is doing; but I have called you friends; for all that I have heard from my Father I have made known to you."

The word "servant" is synonymous with "slave" in this passage. Jesus wants us to think of total obedience, as in the military when a sergeant barks an order and a private jumps. The private may not know why the order has been given and he dare not ask. All he knows is that when the sergeant speaks, he obeys, blindly, immediately.

Notice that Jesus is saying, "*No longer* do I call you servants. . . ." Evidently he once did call the disciples servants, and therein lies a profound message. Servant is a good word in Scripture. Jesus set the tone for the entire evening in the Upper Room by taking the form of a servant and washing the disciples' feet. As William Barclay put it, to be called a slave or a servant of God is a title of honor. Jesus is not trying to disparage the term at all.

Rather he is spelling out a step-by-step process leading to intimacy with him. Friends of the Lord began as servants of the Lord. Friendship is a consequence of obedience.

The Lord called to Abraham telling him to pack his belongings and leave home (Genesis 12:1ff). Abraham obeyed, and set out not knowing where the path would lead. God had sent the marching orders and Abraham marched. James writes, "and the scripture was fulfilled which says, 'Abraham believed God, and it was reckoned to him as righteousness'; and he was called the friend of God" (James 2:23).

We obey the command to love, without knowing the consequences. We do not love because we believe there will be a payoff. We are for one another because Jesus told us to be and, like slaves, we obey the master. It is in that blind obedience that our eyes are opened and we see. Willing to be blind for our Lord's sake, we see as never before.

Let me illustrate. We are all familiar with the episode in Scripture that tells of Jesus on his way to Jerusalem, pausing when he reached the outskirts and weeping over the city. Many people have no concept what to make of that. Why should a grown man cry? Why would the Messiah cry? Was it the pressure? Was it fear? Fatigue? I think not. I think Jesus was living totally the life you and I are called to live, life on the inside, life understanding what Christian love is all about (Luke 19:41-44).

A few years ago I sat in a large dining hall as the York Rescue Mission had its annual banquet. My friend Paul Gorog was the executive director. When his turn to speak came, he began by outlining some of the events of the past year. He then started to relate the stories of some men whose lives were in ruin because of alcohol. In front of four hundred people he burst into tears, but continued struggling to get words out through sobs. As I sat spellbound in my seat, I saw Jesus weeping over Jerusalem.

Maybe our world cannot understand that scene on the outskirts of David's City because our world does not fully know what it means to be radically for each other. Maybe the world will never understand why Paul Gorog cried. But when we really love, when we unconditionally care, then we can't help being moved at the sight of those we love falling into a life that is less than the Lord intends. When they fail, when they reject the promises of Christ, when they choose a living hell instead of heaven on earth, our throats tighten and our eyes grow red. When we care that much, the secret message of the Father turns on like a light within us. We stand with the Lord and see life from the inside through eyes that have been opened by God himself.

Notes

[1]Earl F. Palmer, *The Intimate Gospel* (Waco, Tex.: Word Books, 1978), p. 132.

[2]W. B. J. Martin, "From My Study Window," *Presbyterian Outlook*, vol., 160, no. 33 (September 18, 1978), p. 9.

[3]Albert Schweitzer, *The Quest of the Historical Jesus* (New York: Macmillan, Inc., 1961), p. 403.

CHAPTER 11

The Chosen People

"You did not choose me, but I chose you . . ." (John 15:16).

Remember the audience Jesus had for his last discourse. These were religious survivors. There had been other persons along the way who had heard the message, found it a bit too tough, and opted out. There had been a few well-meaning persons who had applied for discipleship. But they turned out to be unwilling to give up or to alter their life-styles, and Jesus had decided to leave them behind. Still others had hooked up with the band of disciples and traveled about with them for a time before taking offense at some teaching or personal slight and stomping off in disgust. But these hearty souls in the Upper Room had stayed through thick and thin. Where there had been reason or opportunity to leave, they had hung in there. Even when they had not fully understood who Jesus was or what he was up to, they had stuck with him. They were "the company," "the club," "the inner circle," "the survivors."

Yet Jesus was not throwing them an awards dinner or appreciation banquet. He did not give an after-dinner speech thanking them for all they had done for him and meant to him during his earthly ministry. Instead he made a comment that would seem to have been aimed at deflating them by punching a hole in their pride. His comment is at once the most controversial in John 15 and one of the most basic. He looked these rugged survivors right in the eyes and said, "You did not choose me, but I chose you. . . ."

Looking back over previous events, Jesus' words sound like a rather narrow interpretation of what had actually happened. Yes, he had spotted a fisherman by the seashore and offered the initial invitation, "Follow me." But a fisherman would have had quite a bit of latitude in how to respond. He might have said, "I'd love to, but this is not the right time. Call me in a few months." Or, he might have given a very emphatic no! Jesus does not appear to appreciate the role the disciples played in electing to follow him, to say nothing of choosing daily to stay with him. Did he not take their loyalty seriously?

I have wrestled with this troubling issue for months and am now firmly convinced Jesus took his disciples' response very seriously, so seriously that he wanted to give them a lesson to make sure their actions had lasting value. He knew and he knows that staying Christian requires a proper understanding of how we really came to be Christian in the first place. What should I think when I reflect on how I came to this moment of faith? Where should I put my emphasis?

The question boils down to an old theological debate between Arminianism and the Reformed tradition. Arminianism takes its name from Jacobus Arminius, a 16th-century Dutch theologian. He taught that the individual is free to choose his or her own salvation. You are a Christian, he would say, because of the decisions you have made. In the early days of our country, during the first Great Awakening, there was grave concern that the revival might fall prey to the heresy of Arminianism, and heresy was the generally accepted word for it.

Today, however, one could say of Arminianism, "You've come a long way, baby!" Even a casual glance at the contemporary religious scene would reveal that, far from being counted among the heresies, Arminianism is the widely accepted theology of our time. Bill Bright's campaign "Here's Life, America" is vintage Arminianism. Perhaps you saw the bumper stickers with the slogan "I Found It." Critics of the campaign felt that a slogan such as that allowed a person displaying it to take too much credit for faith. "*I* Found It."

The Reformed tradition would paste a different message on the bumpers of its autos. This tradition teaches that when we write our spiritual autobiographies, fewer sentences should begin with "I . . ." and more sentences should begin "The Lord. . . ." Our faith is and has been primarily his doing. "He found me."

Whenever I teach the message of John 15:16 in a discussion group, I can practically guarantee that someone will open a Bible to the Old Testament Book of Joshua. I will hear quoted that well-known passage where the great leader, as an old man, put the issue to the people, calling them to a decision: "Choose this day whom you will serve" (Joshua 24:15). Then the person in the discussion group will quite correctly point out that choosing is always a responsibility for us. And I agree. You and I are supposed to make choices relating to our faith. I have no problem with that. Haven't I already written that we should choose to abide, to pray, and to love? I simply want to present here the larger and more basic picture. We need to recall that when Joshua made his speech about the need to choose, he was addressing the already chosen people. At the deepest level, behind all our human choices, stand the words of our Lord: "You did not choose me. . . ."

Still I get arguments. People insist that they will never accept the Reformed interpretation. "I will never believe that! Of course I chose Christ. I made my decision for him on June 4, 1968 at four o'clock in the afternoon. I am a Christian today because of the decision I made."

John Daane of Fuller Seminary has shared some helpful insights on what is a surprisingly recent phenomenon: the altar call. While I believe an altar call has a valid place, and have worked in crusades that have had altar calls, I am mindful of their dangers. If we teach that a person is claimed by the Lord, and if we want to offer that person a chance to act out publicly what the Lord has done, then altar calls are a legitimate form of worship and praise. But unfortunately the altar call is rarely presented in that light. All too often the call is presented in a way that makes Christianity appear optional. Take it or leave it. A soul fidgets on what one nineteenth-century theologian called "The Anxious Bench," stewing over whether to become a Christian. Crusade leaders often muddy the water by teaching that such a person is a non-Christian as long as he or she remains at the bench. But if that non-Christian makes a decision to come forward, he or she will become a Christian by virtue of arriving at the front. John Daane's point comes into play here. He suggests that it is absurd to believe a non-Christian in a fallen state separated from God is capable of making an ultimate Christian decision, the decision to accept Christ.[1]

In *The Cost of Discipleship,* Dietrich Bonhoeffer wrote that discipleship is not something anybody could or would choose. He posed a theological "Catch-22." If a person claims, "I am going to choose discipleship," that individual, by definition, has no concept of what it means, because anyone who really knew what discipleship entailed would never choose it. Genuine disciples are drafted. Jesus has no volunteer army.[2]

The same truth is echoed in the teachings of people who we might assume would have a high view of our choosing Christianity. Billy Graham wrote in his book *How to Be Born Again,* "A person cannot turn to God to repent, or even to believe, without God's help. God must do the turning."[3]

Keith Miller discusses the psychological dynamics of conversion in his book *The Becomers*. Having quoted Martin Marty's phrase that conversion is like "being grasped," Miller adds, "Inside, it is the feeling of *responding,* not of instigating. One feels that *God* is offering the relationship."[4]

The decision we made, the choice we thought was ours, was really God at work within us. It is impossible to become a Christian without God. Anyone who says, "I am a Christian because I made a decision . . ." may unwittingly be claiming to have become a Christian without God. The testimony implies, "I did it all by myself."

Jesus has another interpretation. We did not do the choosing. He did. As Paul wrote to the Ephesians, "For by grace you have been saved through faith; and this is not your own doing, it is the gift of God—not because of works, lest any man should boast" (Ephesians 2:8-9).

I cannot square Jesus' words "You did not choose me" with the Arminian notion that I chose my own salvation. I stand in the Reformed tradition: "But I chose you." If we want to stay Christian, we had better put a damper on our pride and heap less credit on the bold courageous decision "I made for Christ," and give the praise to Jesus. Base your faith on the decision "Christ made for you."

Ray Lindquist, former preaching minister of the Hollywood Presbyterian Church, has written, "God chooses us not because of what we are, have, have done, or can do, but because of what He is, what He has done, and what *He* can do. God made us, saved us, sustains and secures us. His choice of us is the sovereign expression of His grace."[5] "You did not choose me, but I chose you."

As you read this paragraph, let your mind wander a bit. Think about the significant moments in your spiritual history. Think about the moment when you did make the right decision. Or think of the times you experienced penetrating insight and uplifting inspiration. Think about the time when you sensed the presence and power of God. Think about a moment when you knew you were abiding, or bearing fruit, or allowing the love of Christ to flow through you. Think about that time you woke up to the wonderful fact that you must have been born again because you suddenly knew you were a child of God. Think about those moments which have become building blocks for your faith. Jesus wants us to know that these moments are significant, not because of the outward trappings or the events themselves; they are significant because he was at work in them. "I chose you."

I find that comforting. What a burden is lifted! Do you realize what it means? It means that God is the One who shoulders the responsibility for my faith. This whole thing is his idea. It is his doing, not mine.

If my faith had been my own doing, then a program on how to stay Christian would have to list all the things I had done. I would have to develop my skills to continue doing the same things over and over again. How depressing and exhausting that would be! If I believed I were the deciding factor in my having become Christian, then I would have to conclude that continuing in the faith would demand that I constantly redecide. My perseverance would depend on my own frail and undependable judgment which could be subject to emotional, psychological, and environmental factors beyond my control.

The burden-lifting truth is that Jesus brought me to this moment. What a relief! I can hear him saying to me, "Don't worry how it turns out. Your faith is my decision. Don't be anxious about tomorrow. Let me worry about it."

We can put aside our fears that we might be unworthy of discipleship. We can stop stewing over whether we have what it takes to stay with it. We can stop tossing and turning, worried that God will find out the truth about us and cancel our membership. Jesus is "I am," "the One who generates what is," "the Source." Jesus is the incarnation of the One who has searched us and known us (Psalm 139:1). Jesus has the wisdom of the One who knows our every thought and our every word even before we speak it. He is the One from whom no secrets are hidden and to whom no desires are unknown. He knows our every weakness. I could not pull the wool over his eyes if I wanted to. He knows what he is doing when it comes to you and me. And the Good News from which my exuberance comes is that he is the one who has said to me, "I chose you." He has always known me through and through, and he still chose me. Now that is truly remarkable!

I wonder how the disciples took Jesus' words in the Upper Room. Were they put out that he seemed to be slighting their loyal efforts? I really don't think so. My hunch is that they felt closer to him. They felt more solid in their faith. They felt more secure in their trust of him. I believe they felt the security of resting their faith all the more on Jesus. They had, after all, just been reminded that their faith was his doing in the first place. "You did not choose me, but I chose you."

Notes

[1]John Daane, *Preaching with Confidence* (Grand Rapids, Mich.: Wm. B. Eerdmans, Publishing Co. 1980). pp. 39-43.

[2]Dietrich Bonhoeffer, *The Cost of Discipleship* (New York: Macmillan, Inc., 1961), p. 50ff.

[3]Billy Graham, *How to Be Born Again* (Waco, Tex.: Word Books, 1977), p. 156.

[4]Keith Miller, *The Becomers* (Waco, Tex.: Word Books, 1973), p. 127.

[5]Raymond Lindquist, *Notes for Living* (Phildelphia: J. B. Lippincott Co., 1968), p. 213.

CHAPTER 12

Probable Hatred

"If the world hates you, know that it has hated me before it hated you. If you were of the world, the world would love its own; but because you are not of the world, but I chose you out of the world, therefore the world hates you. Remember the word that I said to you, 'A servant is not greater than his master.' If they persecuted me, they will persecute you; if they kept my word, they will keep yours also. But all this they will do to you on my account, because they do not know him who sent me. If I had not come and spoken to them, they would not have sin; but now they have no excuse for their sin. He who hates me hates my Father also. If I had not done among them the works which no one else did, they would not have sin; but now they have seen and hated both me and my Father" (John 15:18-24).

Many commentators believe the word "if" fails to capture exactly what Jesus had in mind for the beginning of verse 18: "*If* the world hates you. . . . " They believe, as I do, a more definite word is required. Let's see if we can salvage value from the little word, since in most English translations "if" is what we have.

I believe we can do some salvaging, and quite easily. I am convinced that Jesus would nod approvingly at "if" because for all its flaws it at least wards off one insidious threat to Christian living. Think about it. Had the translation been "*When* the world hates you . . . ," most of us Christians would have assumed not only that we would be hated, but that we were supposed to be. We would have begun looking for trouble, trying to stir it up. I can guarantee that I would have done all I could to be the most despised man in town.

That would be silly. We know Christians are not supposed to look for hate; we are to show love. We work for reconciliation rather than division. We exhibit our Christianity by the way we serve the world, not by the way we alienate it. Thank God for giving translators that little word "if." It frees us from having to look for fights.

Come to think of it, the beauty of "if" is its very "iffyness." It says that you and I cannot enter a social situation expecting a definite pattern of response. As we go about our daily lives, people may love us, hate us, ignore us, deceive us, use us, try to change us, or thoroughly misread us. The same act might draw completely opposite reactions from two people we thought were exactly alike. The word "if" says quite boldly, "Who knows how the world might react to us?"

That little word gives two of our fellow Christians endless amounts of unrest. "If" disciplines them because they both have the bad habit of trying to program how people will react to them. Our first friend in the faith never wants to have an enemy, or make anyone angry. He or she supposes that since a Christian is loving, all encounters with others will be amiable. "Smile and the world smiles with you." "If" says, "Don't count on it, Loving Christian." That two-letter adviser of a word informs us that it is practically impossible to be human, to say nothing of following Christ, without rubbing some people the wrong way. No matter how hard a Christian tries to be diplomatic, there just might be angry opposition anyway.

But I suspect we all know our second friend in the faith, the Christian who thrives on conflict. Receiving hate mail and crank calls gets this person's adrenaline flowing. It gives the heady feel of really bugging the secular world with a prophetic message. I have often heard pugnacious disciples boast of what super-saints they must be to have so many people angry at them. But I am suspicious. I cannot help suspecting that some of the so-called secular people are angry at them not because of their faith, but because of their obnoxious way of living it.

Though the word "if" does not fully capture Jesus' thought, it is nonetheless a real blessing to us when we heed its message about not counting on or programming people's responses to us. This is particularly true with negative responses. We can save ourselves many headaches and heartaches by scrutinizing our behavior and weeding out anything, other than honestly living for Christ, that might cause trouble. The reason for stressing this point is that Christians are very frequently accused in conflict of having stirred up the trouble just for the sake of stirring it up. It is shattering to be told we are to blame for trouble and division. In such moments we can find comfort if we can know we did not set out to cause a fight.

A school chum of mine had a rude awakening years ago when he brought a buddy home for leave from the military. Arrangements had been made by phone. The guest room was spruced up and waiting. Everything was set. The whole family looked forward to the visit. Decked out in his uniform, my friend eagerly strutted up the front walk and bounded onto the familiar porch. He could almost see the smiles and feel the hugs before the door swung open. But he met no smiles and got no hugs.

His parents were church members who attended regularly and had sat through many sermons on race relations without even squirming. But they were not prepared for their son to bring a black friend home to sleep in their house. As a sign of the provincialism of the times, the issue had never come up before. When it finally did, the reaction was unfortunate. Not only did the family demonstrate blatant racism, but they also lit into their son, saying the whole mess was all his fault. "It isn't that your friend is black." (It never is.) "It's the way you handled it. You have *deliberately* tried to humiliate us by forcing us into a terrible situation. You are an awful troublemaker." Badly shaken, my friend and his buddy checked into a local motel.

When he told me the story, my pal seemed to be looking for reassurance. He was still being stabbed by guilt feelings. In retrospect he could see that he had been naive in not at least suspecting there could be a problem. And, yes, he did catch his parents by surprise. But it honestly had never occurred to him that skin pigmentation was all that big an issue. After a time in the military he had not really noticed the difference anymore. Now he carried a very deep hurt to think that his parents should believe he would deliberately create a scene at their front door. Their accusation cut him to the core. He was learning in the school of hard knocks that sometimes we go along doing what we sincerely believe is right and we are shocked at how other people unexpectedly jump all over us. The pain was not totally anesthetized in my friend's life; but he began to put things in proper perspective when he accepted the fact that he had not set out to cause trouble.

In verse 18 Jesus begins a thought which he will carry into the first several verses of chapter 16. The subject is opposition, opposition from the world, opposition that bowls us over, opposition that is unnerving, that wears us down. If we are not prepared for it, such opposition can snap our faith, leaving us dangling. Jesus wants us to be forewarned and forearmed. He wants us to know trouble will almost inevitably come our way. This is why "if" does not really say all that Jesus had in mind. Christian, be prepared! Trouble is very, very likely to occur, and for two good reasons.

1. The first reason is in verse 19, where we read "If you were of the world, the world would love its own; but because you are not of the world, but I chose you out of the world, therefore the world hates you." Let's face it, we are not of the world. Christians are not on the same wavelength as other people. I sometimes wonder if church people fully understand or believe that. But it is quite true. Jesus said, "I am not of this world" (John 8:23). "My kingship is not of this world" (John 18:36). How could he say otherwise when this world is so obviously not of him or his kingdom?

Billy Graham received a letter which so moved him that he included it in *Decision* magazine. "Dear Dr. Graham: I was at

Pontiac [Michigan] yesterday. I gave my heart to Jesus. Today we had Show and Tell and I showed my John Bible and I told about giving my heart to Jesus and they laughed at me. I still love Jesus. I am six. I am in the first grade. Love, Eric."[1]

A little boy experienced something so wonderful he wanted to tell his friends all about it. Why shouldn't he? If he had won one hundred dollars in a contest, he would tell them and know they would cheer him and pat him on the back. If he beat up the class bully, they would make a hero of him when he recounted the tale. If he took a trip to Disney World, the class would long to know every detail. Eric merely wanted to share his wonderful Christian experience, and he ran right into the brick wall disciples often hit. The world does not understand.

We Christians see people differently. We give differently. We set priorities differently. We are not content with the power grabbing, the back stabbing, and the pleasure seeking that mark our secular society. Indeed our lives are living indictments of secular values. And people who live by those secular values do not like being indicted.

Take alcohol as an example. While I do not believe a Christian must be a teetotaller, many disciples know themselves called by God to avoid alcohol and sometimes with rather interesting results. Some drinkers are occasionally so abusive that I know of several nondrinkers who "fake it" at parties. By that I mean they ask for tomato juice or a soft drink and doctor the glass to make it look as if they are carrying a mixed cocktail. I sense that beneath the seemingly lighthearted kidding we sometimes hear about how the nondrinker is "really tying one on," having a third diet soda, there may lurk a more menacing script: "I guess you think you are better than I am" or "I guess you think I am drunk." The nondrinker has said nothing. He or she simply asked for a nonalcoholic beverage. The sharp reaction that sometimes comes develops in the mind of the drinker who feels judged and doesn't like it. Nondrinkers often find their invitations to parties dry up.

Rudolf Bultmann offers a sage warning that sometimes the world will hate you in anger, but beware, because they may hate you through enticement and seduction as well.[2] The world will try to assimilate us, water us down, make us acceptable. Many disciples drift from the faith because they do not want to miss out on all the fun promised to those who live worldly lives. Wouldn't it be wonderful to call ourselves Christians and live by worldly standards? Beware: Enticement can be as much a form of hatred as opposition can.

My father once served a church in a town where the local folk made high-quality whiskey and were not afraid to sample their wares. The phone rang in the manse one morning and a lovely voice invited him to come to a party. "Oh, you and Mrs. Galloway *must* come. I'll simply *die* if you are not both there. Say you will. If you don't I'll be *so* disappointed." An unavoidable conflict forced my father to say no, which he did, fearing the disappointment might be more than this poor woman could stand. But he realized almost instantly that she would survive when, as he started to hang up, he could hear a piercing voice shriek, "Yiiipeeeeee! The preacher can't come! Now we can really live it up!" So it goes. Whether they are enticing us or condemning us, our ways are not their ways and when we are honest about it, we all know it.

2. The other reason for animosity toward us goes back to the first verse of John 15 where Jesus said, "I am the true vine." Jesus was making the point that he is authentic, the genuine article. He is the One who feeds us with what is real. We can get a handle on how this might cause problems when I relate an illustration from my own family.

When my two oldest children were quite small, they were peanut butter freaks. They ate gobs of the stuff. One day, as a special treat for them, I went to a place that made genuine peanut butter, directly from the peanuts, right before my very eyes. I raced home with my treasure, feeling quite proud to be such a thoughtful dad. My wife and I watched eagerly as the two youngsters attacked lunch, not knowing what a rare delight awaited them. They roared in unison. "This is yuckie! This isn't peanut butter! Get rid of it!" I was crestfallen.

I am convinced that a primary reason why the world hates Christians is the fact that Christians represent what a genuine human being is supposed to be. While we might wish the world would jump for joy at such a treat, more often they roar, "This is terrible! Get rid of it!" In verses 18, 20, and 21 Jesus builds his case that of course the world will despise us because through him we are in touch with the Creator. There is something authentic happening in us that reminds the world what life was intended to be in the very beginning.

Charlie Shedd wrote a book entitled *The Fat Is in Your Head*. The book is a light look at what makes some people heavy. Shedd's explanation comes down to the fundamental fact that overweight people are out of touch with the Creator. I wonder how much else can be traced to the same root cause—out of touch with the Creator. I wonder how many lives are lived off center, not really in touch with their Source.

The lives of many show that secular life might be tremendously successful but not necessarily fulfilling. An article in the *Manchester Guardian* in 1961 presented something that is just as true today. "The Western world agrees that the good life is based on achievement, success, advance in profession, recognition, wealth, acquisition of the prizes of society." Too many people have become materialism junkies, getting a fix on things, only to realize they are not satisfied, and so they scramble about in search of more things; and unsatisified, they search for even more.

Perhaps a parable for the Western world is the old yarn about the hillbilly who left instructions in his will that he was to be buried sitting up behind the wheel of his brand new Cadillac. For some reason . . . perhaps to create this story . . . his instructions were carried out to the letter. His body was securely placed behind the wheel and the car was slowly lowered down a ramp into the grave. Two of his chums were among the throng that stood nearby. One was overheard saying to the other, "Man, that's really living!"

A life that radiates from a center in touch with the Creator is a constant reminder that many people in this world are surrounded by material comfort, but are spiritually quite dead. One wonders why all these people don't thank us for pointing out their ills and then turn to the more fulfilling life in Christ. Maybe like peanut butter, it is a matter of what a person is used to. Maybe it is just plain old sin. I really don't have an answer. But I do know that given a choice between heaven or hell, some people choose hell. Given a choice between abundant life and living death, some people choose death. Given a choice between the genuine and the phoney, some people will take the phoney every time. That is the way they want it, and heaven help any suggestions to the contrary. In this world the genuine human being was nailed to a cross. It happened to our Lord. When his authenticity shows through us, that same hatred that killed him is turned on us. Sometimes we Christians need to be reminded what happened to our leader.

I believe that Jesus paused after he uttered the words of verse 17. He took a deep breath and scanned the room, making sure that every eye was riveted on him. Then he leaned forward and spoke with an urgent compassion, almost pleading with them to remember. "If the world hates you. . . ."

Christians, if the hatred comes, whether you expected it or it caught you totally by surprise, remember this:

1. Jesus said it would almost certainly happen.
2. If you and I have not been looking for trouble, we need not feel guilty about it.
3. It is the Lord the people really hate.
4. The anger is in the heart of the other person. It is his or her problem. That hate-filled person needs our love and our prayers.

Stay Christian, even if the world hates you.

Notes

[1]*Decision* magazine, April, 1977, p. 11.

[2]Rudolf Bultmann, *The Gospel of John*, trans. G. R. Beasley-Murray, ed. R. W. N. Hoare and J. K. Riches (Philadelphia: The Westminster Press, 1971), p. 549.

CHAPTER 13

Light Causes Shadows

> "If I had not come and spoken to them, they would not have sin; but now they have no excuse for their sin. . . . If I had not done among them the works which no one else did, they would not have sin; but now they have seen and hated both me and my Father" (John 15:22 and 24).

Most of the commentaries I have studied suggest that the best way to understand verses 22 and 24 is to begin with an episode recorded in chapter 9.

Turning back to that chapter, we learn that Jesus and his cohorts had just escaped with their lives from a brouhaha at the temple and were hotfooting it down one of Jerusalem's side streets. Feeling themselves safe at last, their pace slowed. Perhaps looking for an excuse to stop walking and to catch their breath, the disciples decided to make an issue of a man huddled by the side of the road. Something about his manner tipped them off to the fact that he had been born blind. As they stood looking down at him, someone blurted out one of the most insensitive questions in all Scripture. No doubt the strange voice echoed in the darkness of the man's mind. "Rabbi, who sinned, this man or his parents, that he was born blind?" (verse 2).

Jesus answered the question in a way that ministered to the man. "It was not that this man sinned or his parents, but that the works of God might be made manifest in him. We must work the works of him who sent me, while it is day; night comes, when no one can work. As long as I am in the world, I am the light of the world" (verses 3-5).

Jesus then healed the man, using a technique that was sure to get the goat of any legalistic passersby. It was the sabbath. Some of the disciples might have wished Jesus had been more discreet, perhaps whispering inconspicuously in the man's ear something like "In my name be healed." But no; Jesus made quite a show of it. He opted for a pharmaceutical approach, spitting on the ground (an offense to the Jews) and making clay with the spittle. He then placed the clay on the blind eyes and asked the man to wash it off with water from a particular pool, an act that would require his parading through the streets of town with clay on his eyes, a difficult thing to do without being noticed. When the clay was washed away, the eyes began to function. The man could see.

Given little time to celebrate his good turn, the man immediately found himself in the middle of a controversy. He was brought before the Pharisees. Instead of rejoicing with him, their number split right down the middle over a theological question about which the healed man no doubt could not have cared less. Half of the Pharisees insisted that Jesus must be a sinner to have performed such an act on the sabbath. The other half argued that he could not possibly be a sinner or else he would not have been able to perform the miracle in the first place. The squabble left them in a tizzy, unable to react at all.

The public at large was at a loss. So used to seeing the man huddled out of harm's way, they weren't so sure they recognized him walking about, seeing. Perhaps he was an imposter.

The man's parents were questioned. They were so frightened that, though they vouched for the fact that he was indeed their son, they thought the man should speak for himself. Anything to get off center stage would be just fine with them.

So the poor chap was paraded in again for further interrogation by the Pharisees.

What a poignant story; and what a sad commentary on human nature! A man had lived his entire life in darkness. Now for the first time he saw the light of day. In between trips to see the Pharisees, I can imagine he must have jumped for joy. There must have been tears washing through seeing eyes, eyes that saw Mom and Dad for the first time, and began to hook up images with familiar voices. He could see objects he had previously been able only to feel. It was a magnificent moment! A stupendous moment! The power of God had been displayed in human life. And yet there were people who made a stink about it. They could not see God at work. All they saw was a problem which made them hostile. As Helen Keller once expressed it, "Better to be blind and see with your heart than to have two good eyes and see nothing." Some people are spiritually blind. These were the persons who mingled in the crowd near Jesus and murmured against him. These were the people who had the glory of God revealed right in front of them and reacted by plotting Jesus' execution.

A tranquil Jerusalem street had become a scene of bedlam. The healing power of Jesus restored sight to a blind man and at the same time let loose hatred and anger. A godly act stimulated a devilish response. After growing weary of this whole go-round, Jesus pronounced, "For judgment I came into this world, that those who do not see may see, and that those who see may become blind" (verse 39).

With that story as background, let's return to John 15 and look at verses 22 and 24. "If I had not come and spoken to them, they would not have sin; but now they have no excuse for their sin. . . . If I had not done among them the works which no one else did, they would not have sin; but now they have seen and hated both me and my Father."

I must admit that when I first read these words I thought I detected regret in Jesus' tone. I felt he was down on himself, playing the self-pitying game "if only. . . ." "If only I had not come and spoken to them. . . ." I could see him lamenting the anger of the Pharisees, wondering if he had been the cause of it all.

But how wrong I could be! Jesus had no regrets. There is

no anguished "If only . . ." in his mind on this one. He had no second thoughts about having come, performed miracles, taught, separated the wheat from the chaff. How well he knew all along that their hostility and sin were inevitable! It could not be helped. His presence and presence of his followers in this world will always expose latent antagonism toward God. The problem is already there, ingrained in human society. Jesus and his disciples do not create it. Their lives simply reveal it. Jesus restored a man's sight and simultaneously exposed the blindness of the public. His good act revealed their evil nature.

Some years ago our family decided that the sofa in our family room was too much of an eyesore to be left in its present condition. We were embarrassed to have people come into the room with that unsightly sofa staring them right in the face. We made an appointment to have a fellow with a truck come, lug the sofa through the sliding doors, and cart it off for reupholstering. After three weeks of getting used to an empty rectangle several shades lighter than the rest of the floor, we watched as the workmen returned a reupholstered sofa and set it gently back on its spot.

Immediately we loved it! The workmanship was of high quality. My wife had made an excellent selection of material. The children ran their hands over it, hands especially washed for the occasion. My wife and I gingerly sat on it. The verdict was unanimous: a fantastic job!

We decided to step back and drink in the sofa in its surroundings. Now that was a mistake! If you have ever had a piece of furniture redone, you know exactly where I am going with this. All at once we saw for the first time that the lamp on the side table needed to be polished. The table itself did not look so hot. A chair off to the left could use similar reupholstering. The walls looked drab. In fact the whole room looked dingy.

Let's be clear about what happened here and what did not. The reupholstered sofa did not make the room dingy. The room was drab in the first place; only we had never noticed. We had been content to live in a so-so room, until an elegant piece of furniture arrived on the scene and pointed up the truth of the matter. Needless to say, the sofa clashed with its environment.

And Jesus clashed with his. When the light came into the world, he did not cause people to be sinful. They were already sinful. He did not separate them from God. They were already separated, and most of them were quite settled in their separation, thank you. Jesus cast a light on the situation, exposing the dirt and leaving folks without excuse. "The light shines in the darkness, and the darkness has not overcome it" (John 1:5).

I recall an extra-lengthy meeting at church one night. We had prayerfully faced some very hard questions and struggled to make decisions that would honor Christ. When the meeting was over and only one woman remained after everyone else had headed for the parking lot, she paused as if wondering whether to say what was on her mind. "You know, I think this church business would be a lot easier if it weren't for Jesus." She knew exactly what she was saying, and she had a proper attitude behind her words. I had to agree with her. Jesus has a habit of showing up at our committee meetings and shedding his light on our discussion, exposing our shallow efforts to be successful, to draw crowds, to go along with the ethos of our community. He shines his light on the church itself and calls our attention to more and more areas that need to be reformed. He shines in the community, exposing the shenanigans which are so much a part of normal, everyday life. Why, if it weren't for Jesus, we could carry on with business as usual without all the long meetings and heart-wrenching debates.

In our last chapter we dealt with the ominous report that we will very likely get opposition. In this chapter we practically guarantee it. You and I are to let the light of Christ shine in this world, exposing what it will. Suppose our community has fallen into habits and styles diametrically opposed to the teachings of Christ. If we Christians don't bring it to light, who will? If a person we know has been trapped by mind-altering chemicals and we Christians don't shed light on it, who will? If a friend of ours is doing something that could undermine his or her marriage, how can we think it is Christian to pretend we are in the dark about it? Let the light of Christ shine! If our local church has grown spiritually soft, carrying out a hollow routine week in and week out, and some of the members see what is happening, they have a responsibility to bring their revelation to light.

"You are the light of the world. A city set on a hill cannot be hid. Nor do men light a lamp and put it under a bushel, but on a stand, and it gives light to all in the house. Let your light so shine before men, that they may see your good works and give glory to your Father who is in heaven" (Matthew 5:14-16).

I recall sitting in the rear pew of the sanctuary where the presbytery was meeting. The debate was hot. A controversial action had been taken at the national level of our denomination and we at the district level had to figure out how to react. What should we say to the membership that was up in arms, passionately opposed to the denominational action? What should be our response to the persons who had initiated the action? What kind of press release should we draft? One speaker after another marched up to the podium to state his or her case. Before long, the presbytery was developing a rationale constructed to mollify our membership. It looked as though we might be able to calm the troubled waters, keep the attendance up, keep the offerings rolling in. We were moving the issue to the place where we thought the people would buy it. Our marketing skills were in high gear.

Hands were still going up around the room when the moderator called on someone up near the front to my right. A man I recognized as a retired minister strode to the pulpit. He carried his Bible with him. He put the Word of God in front of him, and carefully opened it to the proper passage. He looked up at all of us who were waiting for yet another speech. "Ladies and gentlemen," he intoned, "let's turn to the words of our Lord Jesus and see what he has to say to us today."

The bottom dropped out. When he finished reading from the Sermon on the Mount, we sat in embarrassed silence. The Word had turned a bright spotlight on all of us that afternoon, exposing our fears, our blind ambitions, our willingness to compromise, the ease with which we could twist and distort an issue to keep our churches on a successful track. I thought of the woman who had said the church would be a lot easier if it weren't for Jesus, and I realized anew that an easy church would not really be the church at all. Jesus is our center and he makes it tough sometimes. He did that day, as the air popped out of the balloon we had been blowing up with our own hot air. He did that day, as we took actions that we knew would be hard to interpret, but which we knew the Lord required. Because one saint stood in the fellowship and turned on the light, we could see ourselves and we did not like what we saw. It hurt. Something in us was offended, put out, trying to resist. Had we been merely a crowd assembled from the secular world, we would have let our anger grow. But we knew who we were and whose we were that day. So we changed. Our discussion was born anew, as we let Jesus lead our decision making.

Did you learn this song in Sunday church school?

This little light of mine
I'm gonna let it shine.
This little light of mine
I'm gonna let it shine,
let it shine,
let it shine,
let it shine.

Wherever you are, let it shine, let it shine, let it shine.

CHAPTER 14

We Need the Holy Spirit

"But when the Counselor comes, whom I shall send to you from the Father, even the Spirit of truth, who proceeds from the Father, he will bear witness to me" (John 15:26).

A senior and revered leader of the contemporary church, the late Dr. H. Wheeler Robinson of Oxford, tells us that "in the course of a serious illness, he was led to ask himself why the truths of 'evangelical' Christianity which he had often preached to others now failed to bring him personal strength. They remained true to him, but they seemed to lack vitality. They seemed to demand an active effort of faith, for which the physical energy was lacking. The figure that presented itself at the time was that of a great balloon, with ample lifting power—if only one had the strength to grasp the rope that trailed down from it."[1]

We are nearing the end of our course on how to stay Christian. I suspect there are some readers who have been nodding along through our chapters, saying, "Yes, I agree with that. That makes sense. I buy most of that. But does it really make any difference? When I finish this book, will I actually have what is required to hang on to my faith?"

Other readers may recently have seen a friend or loved one drift from the faith. This book may have been picked up out of fear, as part of a frantic search for a clue as to how to keep from slipping away as well. Where are those readers now? While I would hope all readers have deepened their awareness of discipleship, I know it would be very possible to have come to this point and have only mental images that lack staying power. It would be quite possible to put this book down right now, go out and practice everything we have discussed so far, and lose our faith tomorrow. I find that frightening.

A question may have troubled you from the instant your eye caught a glimpse of our title displayed on a bookshelf. You have no doubt seen more "How to . . . " books than you ever hoped to see in one lifetime. You have probably seen offerings on how to lose weight, how to do home improvements, how to defend yourself, how to become a millionaire. But a book on how to stay Christian has something about it that does not ring true. The title seems to promise a step-by-step set of instructions which, if followed to the letter, would leave us with an indestructible faith. Could we have a money-back guarantee on that? Of course not. (Since I, for one, rise to my level of incompetence trying to follow instructions on how to assemble a child's toy on Christmas Eve, I must admit I feel hopelessly out of my league on something as big as trying to stay Christian.)

And that is just the point. The title is, in a sense, absurd. If, after reading thirteen chapters, you are unsure you have within your grasp the techniques to preserve your faith, join the club. I don't have them either. I cannot stay Christian on my own. Before you sue me for false advertising, let me hasten to add that I believe that what I am now saying has been a conspicuous sub-theme of all that you have read thus far. Until we face the rock-bottom truth that we cannot stay Christian on our own, we will not willingly draw on the resources that are available to us and that can act as preservatives for our faith. Until I was willing to admit that staying Christian was beyond me, I was not ready to ask the Lord's help and mean it. Odd as it sounds, our title, *How to Stay Christian*, makes sense only after you and I admit we cannot stay Christian.

In the Upper Room, Jesus gave last-minute instructions before sending his disciples out into enemy territory. He knew that somewhere in Jerusalem a cross had been built and was lying in silent darkness waiting for its terrible mission. In just a few short hours Jesus' blood would have soaked into that wood, staining it. Ugly holes from torturous spikes would scar the wood, revealing the places where human limbs had been impaled upon it. The cross would have served its purpose. Jesus would be dead.

Then what? Where would the disciples be then? A resurrection, yes, and a brief time to be reunited; an ascension . . . and then what? Could the disciples count on staying Christian in a non-Christian world with Jesus gone? The answer is clear and definite. No! Of course not! Jesus knew that. Jesus knows that. Jesus never expects us to make it on our own.

For this reason, right in the middle of the most threatening statements about how rough it will be for disciples, Jesus refers to the power that can see them and us through. "But when the Counselor comes, whom I shall send to you from the Father, even the Spirit of truth, who proceeds from the Father, he will bear witness to me." These were not words that would catch the disciples by surprise. Rather, they would touch a familiar chord. Instinctively, the disciples' minds would leap back only a few moments to what Jesus had said about the Holy Spirit. They would already know that teachings about the Holy Spirit had provided the lead into what was said about the vine and the branches. Now they would learn why. It is the Holy Spirit who is to be present in Christians' lives, enabling them to endure.

Verses 16 to 31 of John 14 speak for themselves:

> "And I will pray the Father, and he will give you another Counselor, to be with you for ever, even the Spirit of truth, whom the world cannot receive, because it neither sees him nor knows him; you know him, for he dwells with you, and will be in you.
>
> "I will not leave you desolate; I will come to you. Yet a little while, and the world will see me no more, but you will see me; because I live, you will live also. In that day you will know that I am in my Father, and you in me, and I in you. He who has my commandments and keeps them, he it is who loves me; and he

> who loves me will be loved by my Father, and I will love him and manifest myself to him." Judas (not Iscariot) said to him, "Lord, how is it that you will manifest yourself to us, and not to the world?" Jesus answered him, "If a man loves me, he will keep my word, and my Father will love him, and we will come to him and make our home with him. He who does not love me does not keep my words; and the word which you hear is not mine but the Father's who sent me.
>
> "These things I have spoken to you, while I am still with you. But the Counselor, the Holy Spirit, whom the Father will send in my name, he will teach you all things, and bring to your remembrance all that I have said to you. Peace I leave with you; my peace I give to you; not as the world gives do I give to you. Let not your hearts be troubled, neither let them be afraid. You heard me say to you, 'I go away, and I will come to you.' If you loved me, you would have rejoiced, because I go to the Father; for the Father is greater than I. And now I have told you before it takes place, so that when it does take place, you may believe. I will no longer talk much with you, for the ruler of this world is coming. He has no power over me; but I do as the Father has commanded me, so that the world may know that I love the Father. Rise, let us go hence."

The question on which all else turns is Paul's. He put it to some neophyte Christians in Ephesus: "Did you receive the Holy Spirit when you believed?" (Acts 19:2). The Holy Spirit ". . . is God's inspiring breath by which He grants life to creation and re-creation."[2] Or we might say that the Spirit is God in action in human life. It is Jesus in the present tense; or the alter ego of Jesus; or Jesus alive and at work within us. Little wonder that when James Jauncey wrote a book on John 15 he could find no better title for his section on the Holy Spirit than "The Continuing Life."[3] That is exactly what the Spirit gives us.

Thus far our entire journey could be summed up in the selfless words of John the Baptist: "He must increase, but I must decrease" (John 3:30). From the very beginning, when we focused attention on Jesus, the "I am," through varied looks at how we move ourselves from center stage so that he can more fully work through us, we have been setting the stage for the indwelling of the Holy Spirit. In fact, the work of the Spirit could be synonymous with abiding, bearing fruit, loving, and so forth.

The cup of our lives cannot be filled with the Lord until we are willing to empty it of ourselves. This book has attempted to spell out ways for that to happen. But beware lest our piety degenerate into merely an exercise in submissiveness or self-emptying, neither of which has any particular Christian value in itself. The point is not being empty of ourselves. The point is being filled with the Spirit.

One reason why Christians fall away, why churches lack vitality, why disciples come up empty in their hour of testing, is neglect of the Holy Spirit. The quotation with which I began this chapter is taken from the opening paragraph of a book written by Henry Pitney Van Dusen, of Union Theological Seminary in New York. The book, entitled *Spirit, Son and Father: The Christian Faith in the Light of the Holy Spirit,* was his effort to reacquaint the church with its own life support system: the Holy Spirit.

Van Dusen offered a twin definition of the Spirit which tells me, as pastor of a congregation, that the Holy Spirit may be what Christendom needs more than anything right now. He drew on the concepts of potency and intimacy. We Christians live out our discipleship among people who feel powerless. Economic, political, and social forces sweep their lives along and they believe they can do nothing to sway the course they see life taking. Just before sitting down to rewrite this chapter, I heard on a newscast of a woman who had committed suicide because she "felt powerless" against the economic pressures of the day. Again and again I am reminded of an article I read in 1970 on the subject of preaching. The author, whose name I have forgotten, wrote in the conviction that preachers need to address the fact that people feel increasingly powerless. I now firmly believe that we best minister to the feeling of impotence not by telling folks how to win through intimidation or by developing positive, assertive attitudes, but by bringing congregations into the presence of the Holy Spirit and by praying for the Spirit to work in our congregations.

If powerlessness were not enough, I see scores of people who lack any kind of intimate relationship in their lives. Everywhere I turn, another program has been developed to help people develop closer relationships with family, spouses, friends, themselves. And everywhere I turn, I see what the Beatles saw in their song "Eleanor Rigby" about all the lonely people and where they all come from. Ours is a world, ours is a church crying out for the Holy Spirit.

When Jesus mentioned the Spirit in John 15:26, he did so for a very particular reason. For all else the Spirit can do in our lives, the Spirit is the power available to us when we face opposition. Jesus, you will recall, had been explaining how difficult it would be to live for him in a hostile world. We will be hated. Life in Christ will be a confrontation with forces that may very well disorient us. We can come up against so many different approaches to life, all of which badger us and push in on our lives, that we are tempted to throw up our hands and say, "I just don't know what to believe anymore." It is quite possible in this world to drift away from the Christian faith and not even know that we have drifted.

We need the Holy Spirit. Jesus specifically says two things about the Spirit. It is the Spirit of *truth*. He employs that word in this passage because he knows full well that the reality we need most in those harrying moments when we are surrounded by opposing beliefs is truth. We need to have a sense that our lives are holding together from a center that is solid. We need a frame of reference. When our children hit us with whatever new fad has come down the pike; or our friends offer a seemingly brilliant argument to justify godless hedonism; or someone blasts us for the way we have been living our discipleship; and behind the venom is evidence and reasoning that is both godless and perfectly reasonable at the same time, what do we do? How do we know what to think? We turn to the Lord and receive the Spirit of truth.

Jesus almost made himself redundant in driving home the fact that the Spirit comes *from the Father:* ". . . whom I shall send to you from the Father . . . who proceeds from the Father." The truth that Jesus had in mind is true not in the sense that two plus two equals four is true. Truth for him is measured in terms of its relationship to the Source, the Father himself. Because Jesus understood himself as one with the Father, he could say in the Upper Room, "I am . . . the truth" (John 14:6). Our lives radiate truth not by the powers of our brains to deduce rational arguments, but by being in touch with God. The Holy Spirit comes from the Source and makes him real in our lives.

Those last three words are important: ". . . in our lives." In our next chapter we will discuss how you and I are witnesses. Jesus did not mean to imply in verse 26 that the Holy Spirit is a witness to him and that we are also witnesses alongside the Spirit. His purpose was to put the two verses together. The Spirit witnesses to him by using us, and we witness in the power of the Holy Spirit. Jesus pointed out elsewhere that Christians would be hauled in before groups who would put them to the test. "Do not be anxious how or what you are to answer or what you are to say; for the Holy Spirit will teach you in that very hour what you ought to say" (Luke 12:11-12).

Earlier we mentioned that Jesus was giving the disciples input to draw upon when faith was threatened. If your experience is like mine, you sometimes think of just the right words, or recall what you should have done when it is too late to do or say anything. At two in the morning I am brilliant. I remember exactly the argument that would have carried the day in a discussion I had at two o'clock the previous afternoon. If you have had that experience, you might wonder about the mechanism by which these gems from Jesus would come to mind at the exact moment we need them. And Jesus has a ready answer. The technique is prayer, calling on the Holy Spirit to guide us and direct us. The answer is greater openness to the Spirit. I am amazed at the difference that makes. "These things I have spoken to you, while I am still with you. But the Counselor, the Holy Spirit, whom the Father will send in my name, he will teach you all things, and bring to your remembrance all that I have said to you" (John 14:25-26).

A spirit-filled Christian was the guest on a talk show a few years ago. Her appearance was the result of jokes having been made at her expense on a previous show. Throughout the interview the host was most gracious, and yet on another wavelength. Though I respect the way he handled the conversation and admire his wit, that dialogue with a spirit-filled Christian hit me and several of my friends as a parable of the role the Holy Spirit plays in this world. The talk show host was glib; but the guest was genuine. Her being in touch with the Source came through. The host was self-consciously, and I believe deliberately, superficial, sensing a need to keep his audience. The guest did not care about ratings. She was expressing the insight that welled up within her as a result of her being in touch with Truth. The host was clever. The guest's words were often clever, too. But there was more. We were not struck by the brilliance of her mind, or by how well she had prepared for debate. What came across to us was that her life was in tune with a level of reality that spoke of ultimate things. Her life rested on a profoundly powerful truth.

As you might imagine, the audience for the show was not instantly converted, nor did they seem all that impressed with what she said or the way she said it. In fact, they seemed to feel that the guest was downright peculiar. The Holy Spirit does not work in us so that we can wow the world. The Spirit works to bring the Truth to light through us, and that does not go over very well with some audiences. But the Spirit has another agenda: holding us together and keeping us in touch with the Source of our lives. I ask no more.

Jesus knew we would not be able to stay Christian on our own. So he said, "I will not leave you desolate" (John 14:18). Always true to his word, he has sent his Holy Spirit. The Holy Spirit is God's strategy to keep us Christian in an unfriendly world. We can close with an axiom: "Without the Spirit we will not be able to stay Christian. With the Spirit we will." It's as simple as that.

Notes

[1] Henry Pitney Van Dusen, *Spirit, Son and Father: The Christian Faith in the Light of the Holy Spirit* (New York: Charles Scribner's Sons, 1958), p. 9.

[2] Hendrikus Berkhof, *The Doctrine of the Holy Spirit* (Atlanta: John Knox Press, 1977), p. 14.

[3] James H. Jauncey, *The Compelling Indwelling* (Chicago: Moody Press, 1972), pp. 113-123.

CHAPTER 15

Called to Witness

". . . and you also are witnesses, because you have been with me from the beginning." (John 15:27).

I am often asked if I get nervous when I preach. "Isn't it scary to get up there all by yourself in front of all those people?"

The question takes me back to the days when I was still living under my parents' roof and attending the church where my father was the preacher. I often asked him if he were nervous in the pulpit. As his son, I knew I was nervous for him, at times being so jittery about the possibility of his making an embarrassing mistake that going to church at all was a major strain. I did everything possible to avoid having to attend. His assurances did not penetrate my irrational fear. He told me he had no fear about preaching. His only worry centered on getting the choir into their places on time, and being sure the ushers knew what to do. I could never understand how a person could be so calm in the pulpit. How could he not be scared stiff about losing his voice, or losing his place, or saying the wrong word? He assured me that all these things can happen and had happened to him. But he was completely unperturbed by them.

It was not until I had been called to my own church and began to preach every Sunday that I understood what he meant. Part of my nervousness wore off because I grew accustomed to preaching. But that was not the whole story.

I have heard people say that a preacher ought to be nervous. It gets the energy flowing. I disagree. A preacher should be excited about the message, and eager to share it. But nervousness, as I understand the word, is improper. People who argue that we preachers should be nervous are thinking about an actor or actress getting ready for a performance on Broadway where nervous energy can be beneficial. But preaching is not a performance. It is sharing God's word. As a teenager I worried what people would think of my father as a preacher. Now, whenever I try to "look good," or sound like a "prince of the pulpit," or impress myself with how perceptive and courageous I can be, I am tight as a drum mounting the pulpit steps. I have discovered that my nerves are on edge to the extent that I am worried about my own image. This tightness, I believe, is God's way of telling me I am not prepared to witness. Witnessing is like abiding. It is like loving. It is like bearing fruit. It is letting the reality of Jesus Christ happen through us. My nerves are for me a barometer of whether I am putting out the gospel according to Galloway, or whether I am allowing myself to be used in the service of Christ's gospel.

When the Holy Spirit has taken hold of our lives and turned our energies to his service, the human instrument ceases to be the issue. So what if I get my tongue tied. So what if I break into a hacking cough. I hope the congregation will not be distracted. They know they are not there to worship me anyway. They understand that I am only human. The focus is on the Lord.

I guess the best answer I have for the people who ask if I get nervous standing up there in the pulpit all by myself is that I don't stand up there all by myself. Unless the Holy Spirit is with me, speaking through me, I ought not to be up there in the first place. And, yes, if I did have to stand up there all by myself, you would never be able to get me anywhere near a pulpit.

When Jesus told the disciples, ". . . you are witnesses," he had already told them about the Holy Spirit. The sequence is important. The Acts of the Apostles is summed up in the eighth verse of chapter 1: "But you shall receive power when the Holy Spirit has come upon you; and you shall be my witnesses in Jerusalem and in all Judea and Samaria and to the end of the earth." Jesus instructed his disciples at the ascension to wait and pray for the Holy Spirit. Then in the power of the Spirit they would witness to him.

It would happen naturally. Someone once wrote that Paul never gave the early church a pep talk about evangelism. He really had no need to. That would be like giving a football team a pep talk on the need to clean up their plates at the training table after practice. While there is some question whether an imperative or indicative occurs in the original (in John 15:27), most commentators admit it makes no difference. Spirit-filled Christians are hungry to get on with it. Jesus needs only to say, "You *are* my witnesses." When the Holy Spirit is at work in us, we can't help but live lives that bring Jesus to life so that he becomes real for those around us.

A popular story has it that years ago a well-known New York City preacher invited an evangelist to deliver the morning sermon. This was a daring move because the church was self-consciously quite fashionable and accustomed to hearing a high level of sophistication from its pulpit every week, and this particular evangelist was quite conspicuously a "hayseed." Well, the day arrived and the sermon began. To the utter horror of everyone present, the evangelist slaughtered the English language, mispronounced well-known biblical names, and carried on in an accent that was strictly from the sticks. The congregation stirred and fidgeted in discomfort, showing as much annoyance as their own protocol would permit in church. The man in the pulpit just kept on belting out his sermon, regardless.

About six or seven minutes into the message, something happened. A hush came over the room. Members of the congregation seemed frozen in rapt attention. No longer did they notice the accent, or the mispronunciations, or the bad grammar. In fact, no longer did they notice the preacher at all. It was as though their ears were attuned to another Voice speaking to them from beyond, a Voice that chose that day to use the visiting preacher as a mouthpiece.

The congregation experienced in that moment what our churches need. We do not need more meetings to clutter our already crowded schedules and keep us out even more nights. What the church needs is a meeting with its Lord. Meeting is more important than meetings. The purpose of witnessing is for people to meet Jesus.

I believe that the tense of Jesus' words carries a message. "You are witnesses." That is present tense. It has a "right at this moment" meaning to it. Jesus could have said, "When we break up and I send you out into the world, then you will become witnesses." At the close of Matthew's account, Jesus did give that kind of message (Matthew 28:19). But in the last discourse recorded in John 15 there is a here-and-now quality that we dare not overlook. Jesus wanted his disciples to know that they had and would always have a challenge to witness to each other. Witnessing is not simply making Christ real to those outside the faith; witnessing is also keeping Christ real for those of us on the inside.

A friend of mine once confided in me how stunned he was when a fellow church member used the Lord's name in a faithful sense at a dinner party. Evidently the guests, all of whom were Christians, had begun to discuss future plans when this one man had chimed in that "the Lord" was calling his family to do something. My friend was used to hearing people give any number of reasons for their intentions. But hearing someone come right out at a social gathering and claim that the Lord played a role was brand new. While he was hardly the type of chap to relish religious jargon, his consciousness was raised on this one. He suddenly saw that Jesus is indeed Lord in our homes, on our jobs, and at our dinner parties. A Christian had witnessed to a Christian.

Have you ever watched a baseball game and noticed that when a runner gets to first base he has a chat with the first-base coach? I cannot tell you verbatim what is being said, and probably could not get it printed even if I knew. But I know the gist. I can guarantee you that the coach is not trying to come up with something the runner has never heard before. Novelty is irrelevant. The coach is not trying to look insightful or intelligent. His job is to go over the obvious. Make sure the runner is aware of what he ought to have known anyway: how many are out; what to do on certain types of plays that might come up. Good baseball teams communicate with one another, going over the obvious facts, making sure that everyone is concentrating on the basic issues. We disciples need to learn how to coach first base.

I believe a dramatic revolution would sweep through our congregation if we regularly reminded one another to be more loving, if we systematically kept the reminder before us that Jesus is our Lord and Savior. Unhappily we are often afraid to tell old stories, or share what we think people have already heard, and so we keep quiet. Then, Christians we thought were sure in their faith drift away and we discover too late that we should have been witnessing to them all along. We don't stay Christian by hearing only new and excitingly different ideas. We stay Christian by feeding on the meat and potatoes of the faith.

I love to tell the story,
For those who know it best
Seem hungering and thirsting
To hear it, like the rest.

The Holy Spirit is the great leveller and the great excuse killer. Many Christians try to beg off on this witnessing business. They do not feel qualified. They wonder why they should witness when others are so good at it. Of course there are some persons who have eloquent speaking ability and there are others who can think in a way that permits them to express the truth of Christ in graphic language, and there are still others who have a knack for leading groups in courageous social witness. We can thank God for such individuals. But the Spirit is saying to all of us, "Don't sit back and let these people do all the work. You are witnesses, too." A humble heartfelt expression inspired by the Spirit can do more in God's plan than the most eloquent sermon or courageous public witness. No matter what your weaknesses, or your reputation, or your fear and trepidation, the Spirit can use you, plans to use you, will use you. "You are my witnesses." That means you.

. . . Or does it? Right at the very end of John 15, Jesus said something that could give us the impression that we are excluded from everything he had said up to that point. "And you also are witnesses, *because you have been with me from the beginning.*" From the days when he walked along the seaside recruiting followers, they had been with him. They had been at his side throughout his ministry. Alas, you and I were born nineteen hundred years too late to have shared in those moments. Do we conclude that the teachings about abiding, bearing fruit, loving, and witnessing are directed exclusively to the fellowship in the Upper Room and are for their ears only? Not at all.

To get quite literal about it, the disciples had not been with Jesus "from the beginning" any more than we have. John begins his Gospel, "In the beginning was the Word, and the Word was with God, and the Word was God. He was in the beginning with God; all things were made through him, and without him was not anything made that was made" (John 1:1-3). This Word was made flesh (John 1:14) in the person of Jesus. The disciples were not in on any of that. They did not appear on the scene until Jesus was thirty years old, and the creation was . . . well, I don't know how old.

William Temple has written, "We were baptized in infancy; we were (by God's great mercy and election) brought up in Christian homes. Not from the beginning of His ministry, but from the beginning of our lives, we are with Him."[1] Other commentators teach that you and I share with the disciples in the Upper Room an experience with the Holy Spirit and the Spirit always makes Christ contemporary. The disciples knew the Lord in their time and we know him in our time. It is fair to say that you and I witness to the Lord, because we have been with him from the beginning of our own journey with him.

I know myself to have been with him from the beginning in another sense. In the Holy Spirit I am a part of a mission that has been growing since the first Pentecost and will expand to the end. The mission of the Spirit begins with Christ and explodes from the One to the many. I am a Christian because I am a part of that explosion, that movement, that mission and ministry. I am immersed in a flow that began at Pentecost and will move right up to the last day.

One of the most significant events in my ministry was receiving a call from the First Presbyterian Church of York, Pennsylvania. I slaved over the sermons which their pulpit committee would hear. I geared up for the interviews. For weeks I fretted and sweated over the ordeal. Travelling from what was then my home in upstate New York to Baltimore, where the committee would hear me preach, I made a loop through Cambridge, New York, to visit my ninety-five-year-old grand mother. Her hearing and eyesight were practically gone. But her heart was sound and so was her mind, which was a storehouse of spiritual wisdom and power. We sat on a swing which hung from the ceiling of the front porch. There we conversed, she speaking in normal tones and I shouting at the top of my lungs. After a bit, she put her hand on my knee and said, "Don't worry. You will get the call and have a marvelous ministry there." My fears were calmed. I knew she was right. I could not figure out why they would call me or how I would ever be able to lead a church so large. But I knew I had heard the words of one in touch with the Truth. As history records, she was right.

This is but one example of how the power of the faith crosses generations, holding us in larger fellowship. I was in touch with a person two generations past. The power of her time touched and empowered my time. I felt like Timothy to whom it was written, "I am reminded of your sincere faith, a faith that dwelt first in your grandmother Lois and your mother Eunice and now, I am sure, dwells in you" (2 Timothy 1:5). I know that I live in the same fellowship with my grandmother who now lives in heaven. I live in the fellowship of Luther, and Calvin, and Augustine, and Paul, and John, the beloved disciple, and countless Christians yet to be called. As a part of the church, we have been with Jesus from the beginning. And we will be with him at the end. As someone once said, "The man who has lost faith in the ultimate victory of the church has lost faith in God."

I can stay Christian because I know that even if I fail, the Church will not fail. The powers of death shall not prevail against it (Matthew 16:18). Even if my efforts at abiding, and loving, and witnessing come to nothing in my time and place, I know that around the world thousands have become Christians while you have been reading this book. The church is on the move. Christendom is alive and growing. By the power of the Holy Spirit you and I will stay Christians and know ourselves to be part of a company of believers that can never be stopped.

> Faith of our fathers! living still
> In spite of dungeon, fire, and sword,
> O how our hearts beat high with joy
> Whene'er we hear that glorious word:
>
> Faith of our fathers! God's great power
> Shall win all nations unto thee;
> And through the truth that comes from God
> Mankind shall then be truly free:
>
> Faith of our fathers! we will love
> Both friend and foe in all our strife,
> And preach thee, too, as love knows how
> By kindly words and virtuous life:
>
> Faith of our fathers, holy faith!
> We will be true to thee till death.
>
> (Frederick W. Faber)

Notes

[1]William Temple, *Readings in St. John's Gospel* (London: Macmillan, Inc., 1940), p. 276.

Epilogue

A way to measure the effectiveness of Jesus' teaching is to examine what became of the persons who heard the last discourse. Did they fall away or did they stay Christian?

The investigation is not without problems. We do not have exact agreed-upon information available to us on the eleven disciples.* Tradition has spun out several legends on the same person, sending him in different directions at the same time, suggesting different ways he might have died. But on one thing there is unanimous accord: Not one of the eleven disciples quit on his faith. They all stayed Christian to the end.

*There is reason to believe that more than eleven persons heard Jesus' final discourse. Many persons, in addition to the twelve disciples, traveled with him, and would naturally have joined him in celebrating the Passover. There is further question whether the discourse took place in the Upper Room or while walking through the streets of Jerusalem. The last words before chapter 15 were "Rise, let us go hence." I believe they lingered for Jesus' last teaching. It is not until the first verse of chapter 18 that we get the idea the group was actually on the move. Throughout this book I have built on the assumption that neither issue really matters. Neither affects the content of the teaching. I have therefore painted the picture of Jesus in the Upper Room with his eleven disciples, and left it at that, so that we could concentrate on the content of his message.

The only point where tradition is hazy comes when it tries to explain exactly how a particular disciple continued to abide, to bear fruit, to love, to witness to Jesus.

Admitting that some educated guesswork (with an emphasis on guesswork) is required, let's track what happened to the eleven.

Simon Peter—Denied Jesus three times. Was especially sought out by Jesus after the resurrection. Became a leader in the early church. Contributed to the New Testament writings. Acted as a missionary, being martyred in Rome, probably crucified upside down.

James, Son of Zebedee—Became the first of the disciples to be martyred. In A.D. 44 was executed by Herod who sought to increase his popularity by killing the most conspicuously committed follower of Jesus. Was chopped in half in Jerusalem.

Andrew—Became a missionary to Russia, Greece and Turkey. Was crucified on an X-shaped cross, tied with cords to prolong the agony.

Philip—Had a powerful ministry. Was hanged, upside down, facing Nathanael (Bartholomew). Prayed and pleaded that he be allowed to die but that his friend be released.

Nathanael (Bartholomew)—was released from execution attempt. Faith remained stronger than ever. Was missionary to India. Chopped to death in Armenia.

Simon the Zealot—Missionary to Persia and perhaps Britain. Probably died a violent death involving either a battle-ax or a saw.

James, Son of Alphaeus—Reputed to have looked so much like Jesus that Judas had to kiss the Lord so that the authorities would not arrest the wrong man. Fasted until he saw the Risen Christ. Taken to a high tower, ordered to renounce Jesus. Instead he preached Christ. Was thrown down. Survived. Was stoned by the crowd. Finally died when struck on the head by a club wielded by a fuller.

Thaddaeus (Judas, Son of James)—Carried out extensive healing ministry. Died of wounds from arrows.

Matthew—Left permanent record of Jesus' life and ministry. Was a missionary to many lands. Martyred, with several gruesome methods of execution being listed.

Thomas—Carried out a most effective ministry in India until martyred, by being pierced by a lance.

Ten men gave their lives to Jesus Christ. Ten men were faithful to the bitter, painful end. "If you were of the world, the world would love its own; but because you are not of the world, but I chose you out of the world, therefore the world hates you" (John 15:19).

John, the beloved disciple—Contributed to the writings of the New Testament. Often arrested and held in captivity. Returned to Ephesus where, as a weakened, feeble old man, he ministered until his death.

And . . . Jesus of Nazareth—Executed as a common criminal the day after dining with his disciples in the Upper Room. Buried. Raised from the dead. Ascended into heaven. Will return at the end of it all. By the power of the Holy Spirit is with us now helping us to stay Christian.